business *masterminds*

stephen
COVEY

ROBERT HELLER

A Dorling Kindersley Book

Dorling  Kindersley

LONDON, NEW YORK, SYDNEY, DELHI, PARIS,
MUNICH & JOHANNESBURG

Senior Editor Adèle Hayward
Senior Art Editor Caroline Marklew
DTP Designer Jason Little
Production Controller Sarah Coltman

Senior Managing Editor Stephanie Jackson
Managing Art Editor Nigel Duffield

Produced for Dorling Kindersley by
Grant Laing Partnership
48 Brockwell Park Gardens,
London SE24 9BJ
Managing Editor Jane Laing
Project Editor Frank Ritter
Project Art Editor Steve Wilson

First published in Great Britain in 2001
by Dorling Kindersley Limited,
9 Henrietta Street, London WC2E 8PS

2 4 6 8 10 9 7 5 3 1

A CIP catalogue record for this book is
available from the British Library

ISBN 0 7513 1278 9

Reproduced by Colourpath, London
Printed in Hong Kong by Wing King Tong

see our complete catalogue at
www.dk.com

Author's Acknowledgments
The many sources for this book have been
acknowledged in the text, but I must now
express my great debt to everybody, above
all to the Mastermind himself. Nor would
the book exist but for the inspiration and
effort of the excellent Dorling Kindersley
team – to whom my warm thanks.

Packager's Acknowledgments
Grant Laing Partnership would like to
thank the following for their help and
participation:
Index Kay Ollerenshaw
Picture Research Andy Sansom

Picture Credits
The publisher would like to thank the
following for their kind permission to
reproduce the following photographs:
Corbis UK Ltd: 82; Catherine Kamow 102;
Robert Holmes 45; **Courtesy of Franklin
Covey Company:** 1, 4, 107; **Katz Pictures:**
Jim Leynse/Sara Rea 27; Steve Labadessa
9; **Popperfoto:** 16; **Frank Spooner
Pictures:** John Rogers 72; **The Stock
Market:** John Paul Endress 52;
Tony Stone Images: Adam LuBroth 23;
Christopher Thomas 92; Jon Gray 59;
Lori Adamski Peek 28; **Telegraph
Colour Library:** Jeri Gleiter 12;
Times Syndication: 75

Front jacket: **Courtesy of Franklin Covey
Company**

Contents

The business evangelist

Stephen R. Covey is the most successful of the American gurus who use psychological and spiritual insights to inspire managers (and many other kinds of readers) to improve their performance and transform their lives.

The phenomenal response to Covey worldwide is just as significant as the ideas themselves. His book, *The Seven Habits of Highly Effective People*, published in 1989, has sold 10 million copies and won the author an unparalleled audience, ranging from private individuals to global corporations. Covey has tapped a widely felt need to believe that material achievement is founded on following clear, transferable, personal moral principles. His teaching, which reflects Covey's Christian beliefs as a devout Mormon, is grounded in practicality – like Covey's own career.

A powerful speaker, he has spread his ideas through seminars, consultancy, many media, and his own multinational organization, now Franklin Covey, Inc. But the core of all these activities lies in *Seven Habits*, with its emphatic insistence that individuals are moral beings who are in control of their own destinies, and that unselfish self-help is the path to worldly success.

Robert Heller

Biography

Stephen R. Covey was born in Utah of Mormon stock in 1932. His career was originally academic. Armed with an MBA from Harvard and a doctorate from Brigham Young University (BYU), in the Mormon heartland of Utah, he taught organizational behaviour as a professor in the latter institution. The MBA not only brought a solid business background to his teaching, it also developed valuable skills. In the businesslike but theocratic setting of BYU he showed considerable organizational talent, acting as director of university relations and assistant to the president. The current BYU president, Merrill J. Bateman, exemplifies the same Mormon dualism; he was previously, among many other things, a Mars, Inc. executive and Presiding Bishop of the Mormon Church.

Inspired by Mormon belief

The Mormon Church of Jesus Christ of the Latter-day Saints has had a huge influence on both Covey's career and his thinking. For a start, it is difficult not to see a strong connection between the "13 fundamental beliefs" set out by the Church and the "seven habits" explained in his blockbuster, *The Seven Habits of Highly Effective People* (1989). Mormonism must be the source of Covey's belief that there are fundamental, unarguable principles, which have a defined number. Some of the beliefs, such as the thirteenth, "We believe in being honest, true, chaste, benevolent, virtuous, and in doing good to all men," have direct relevance to Covey's own gospel of personal, interpersonal, and organizational effectiveness.

Covey can claim to be one of the most successful educators in history: by his own account, his student body is numbered in the millions. He very often quotes the Chinese philosopher Lao Tzu, and his "timeless adage": "Give a man a fish and you feed him for a day; teach him how to fish and you feed him for a lifetime." The knowledge he gained through teaching persuaded Covey that people could improve themselves radically if only they understood how to make those improvements happen.

Voice of enlightenment

But Covey's rider to Lao Tzu's wise words has been just as important in his career: "Develop teachers of fishermen, and you lift all society". Like his evangelical predecessors, Covey seeks to lift individuals into enlightenment so that their families, their organizations, their whole society will follow them along the paths of righteousness. Just like St. Ignatius Loyola with his Jesuits, Covey has created disciples and an organization that can spread the word far more widely than a lone individual, even one as amazingly industrious as himself.

Here his business abilities and his Harvard MBA have proved highly effective. Covey left BYU to found Stephen R. Covey and Associates and fulfil his ambition of having a major influence on American management. With a handful of associates, Covey developed the firm rapidly to the point where major worldwide expansion was feasible. In 1984 he took his commercial activities into a new management training organization, named the Covey Leadership Center. Thirteen years later this merged with Franklin Quest, famous for its time-managing Planner, to become Franklin Covey Company, of which he is co-chairman today.

His chairman partner is Hyrum W. Smith. Theirs is a thriving public company, traded on the New York Stock Exchange since 1997, with over 4,000 staff or "members". There are 128 Franklin Covey Seven Habits retail stores, mostly selling the company's products in North America, but also found in some 30-plus other countries. Translated into 28 languages, the Covey products have carried the message of this latter-day evangelist around the world. Each year the members train more than 750,000 people, and help to sell over 1.5 million books. The huge sales (over 10 million copies of *Seven Habits* alone) contribute heavily to a turnover in excess of $550 million.

Spreading the word

In total, Franklin Covey has 15 million books in print, with all other titles dwarfed by the blockbuster *The Seven Habits of Highly Effective People*. Published in 1989, when Covey was in his mid-fifties, *Seven Habits* has spawned dozens of offshoots, in both book and electronic form. But the company's activities have ramified far beyond training and books. Its facilities in the Rocky Mountains of Utah, where Covey and his wife live, "empower" trainees to spread the Covey doctrine around the world – together with the products that apply the ideas to individuals, organizations, and families.

Covey has actually written more about the family than business; *The Seven Habits of Highly Effective Families* (1998), like its model, has spawned many derivatives, from *The Seven Habits Family Journal* to *Balancing Work and Family* (both 1998). A deep belief in the family and its values is fundamental to Mormonism. In Covey's work, it appears not only in his writings on the family, but in his philosophy at large. Yet, despite their very substantial personal and ethical content, Covey has no doubt that his major non-family works are definitely "business books".

The evangelism, in fact, is thoroughly businesslike. That commercial emphasis explains why Franklin Covey's clients include all but 18 of the 100 biggest American companies by sales, and two-thirds of the top 500. The corporate clients, including many organizations operating on a much smaller scale, are offered consulting, personal coaching, and on-site training; or they can send people to the workshops that the company conducts in over 300 cities – again, outside as well as inside North America. There are also more than 7,000 "licensed client facilitators" whose mission is to teach the Franklin Covey curriculum.

Family man
Drawing much of the inspiration of his books from experiences within his family and marriage, Stephen Covey has found an avid readership in the international business community.

The interest that Covey has evoked in management is essentially pragmatic. As he says in his book, *The Seven Habits of Highly Effective People*, "helping individuals, organizations, and families become more effective" meets the desire of companies to attain higher productivity from self-motivating employees. Management Covey-style seeks to align individual and corporate aims, not only through agreed plans and targets, but through personal development. Covey is unique among management gurus in treating personal and public virtue as one and the same.

Other gurus have tended to concentrate on either improving the individual or improving the organization. Covey presents them as inseparable – and his own business success supports his argument. Just as Franklin Covey qualifies its founder as a teacher of corporate executives, so his family life supports his authority on matters of family management. Covey and his wife Sandra have nine children, and he proudly describes himself, above all other distinctions, as "husband, father, and grandfather".

Philosophy of achievement

Child-bearing and rearing apart, the principles that Covey has espoused so successfully are normally associated with other-worldly, spiritual lives. But Covey's pride and pleasure over the progress of a previously disappointing son (see p. 26) are based on the same material achievements that would lead any pushy, over-identifying, purely secular parent to boastfulness. Thus, after Covey changed his parental tactics and strategy to what developed into the Seven Habits philosophy, the under-achieving boy "was elected to several student leadership positions, developed into an all-state athlete, and started bringing home straight A report cards". Covey concluded that the change of philosophy that worked so well with Covey Jr. offered the same hope to everybody: you can be true to yourself and still achieve what you want.

Better still, goodness and success fed off each other. The other abiding element that emerged from this experience with his son was the idea that the family is a source of more widely applicable wisdom. Covey's books make liberal use of other anecdotes from his children's upbringing and his relationship with his wife – and relatively little use of anecdotes culled from identified businesses.

Drawing income from wisdom

The identification of family truths with performance factors in larger organizations is at the core of Covey's thought and practice. His writing and commercial activities have promulgated these ideas in a purely secular context – and with excellent commercial results for Covey himself. The Mormon readiness to serve God and also make money suits him well, for Mormons truly see no conflict: serve God well, and your business will also succeed.

Covey's own career, while inspired by religion, has been marked by many secular distinctions; in 1996 he was named by *Time* magazine as one of the top 25 Most Influential Americans. That same year he was cited by the magazine *Sales and Marketing Management* as among the top 25 Powerbrokers. As a successful businessman, Covey has very few peers among the ranks of the management gurus: nor can many match his success as a preacher. Practising what he preaches has worked well enough for Covey in person to serve as evidence that, at least for some people, the Seven Habits actually work – highly effectively.

1

Building basic effectiveness

The importance of ensuring the long-term production of golden eggs ● Why integrating basic, enduring principles into your character leads to true personal and business success ● **Exploiting the freedom to choose how you will respond to stimulus** ● The Seven Habits that make people highly effective ● **Developing the Seven Habits from dependence to independence and then interdependence** ● How to achieve the correct P/PC balance between Production and Production Capability

Stephen Covey's fundamental thought is simple but powerful. He believes that "there are basic principles of effective living... people can only experience true success and enduring happiness as they learn and integrate these principles into their basic character."

Covey calls this teaching "the Character Ethic", basing it on "natural laws in the human dimension that are just as real, just as unchanging, as unarguably 'there' as laws such as gravity are in the physical dimension." Covey regards this statement as an "objective reality". The natural laws "are woven into the fabric of every civilized society throughout history." They "comprise the roots of every family and institution that has endured and prospered."

Character versus Personality

Covey distinguishes the Character Ethic from what he calls "the Personality Ethic" – a more complex idea, for which he has no such clear and simple definition. In contrast to the Character Ethic's "principle-centred" philosophy, the Personality Ethic is concerned only with practicalities. It embraces all efforts to "change outward attitudes and behaviour", with emphasis on the "outward". Covey does not suggest that such efforts are invariably futile. On the contrary, some of the Personality Ethic's elements – "personality growth, communication skill training, and education in the field of influence strategies and positive thinking" – are beneficial, "in fact sometimes essential for success". But Covey regards even the essentials contained within this Ethic as secondary, and "secondary traits alone have no permanent worth in long-term relationships".

Moreover, the search for short-term fixes is eventually self-defeating. He argues: "If there isn't deep integrity and fundamental character strength, the challenge of life will cause true motives to surface and human relationship failure will replace short-term success." To Covey, the contrasting value of obedience to the natural laws is not open to argument:

"Principles are guidelines for human conduct that are *proven* [my italics] to have enduring, permanent value.... They are essentially unarguable because they are self-evident."

Covey's Character Ethic has a close fit with Christian ideals. He denies that his ideas are "esoteric, mysterious, or 'religious'", asserting that, while not one of them is "unique to any specific faith or religion, including my own", they all play "a part in most every major enduring religion, as well as enduring social philosophies and ethical systems".

Changing character

Covey opposes most psychologists by arguing that changing one's character is just as feasible as changing behaviour. There is an evident problem here. Clearly, being faithful, temperate, just, or industrious are behaviours. The extent to which people behave in these worthy ways is governed by their personalities, which, scientists would say,

---

"The essence of principle-centred living is making the commitment to listen to and live by conscience. Why? Because of all the factors that influence us in the moment of choice, this is the factor that will always point true north."
First Things First (1994)

Hollywood insight

Cecil B. DeMille commented during the making of his epic film
The Ten Commandments: *"It is impossible for us to break the*
law. We can only break ourselves against the law."

are created by heredity and experience, nature and nurture.
Covey rejects the concept that, like the dogs famously
researched by the Russian physiologist Ivan Pavlov
(1849–1936), men and women are conditioned to "respond
in a particular way to a particular stimulus". Rather,
mankind has a unique ability: *"Between stimulus and*
response, man has the freedom to choose." The italics are
Covey's. This gap between stimulus and response is key to
Covey's thinking. By the exercise of independent will,
people can act on their self-awareness, "free of all other
influences". They can exploit imagination and obey the
promptings of conscience, which Covey defines as "a deep

inner awareness of right and wrong, of the principles that govern our behaviour". This philosophy will have none of the view (which is, however, perfectly tenable) that the qualities exalted by Covey are also conditioned by heredity and experience. That view is what he calls a paradigm, "the way we 'see' the world... in terms of perceiving, understanding, interpreting". Covey says that "we have many, many maps in our head", divided mostly between maps of "the way things are, or realities, and the way things should be, or values". These maps are indeed conditioned. But, argues Covey, shift the paradigm, change the map, and you alter attitudes, behaviours, and relationships.

Shifting the paradigms

This is the essence of Covey's teaching, and of his appeal. Human beings, whether as individuals or when gathered together, have problems, which they naturally wish to solve. They want to be better spouses, parents, employees, employers, and so on. Covey teaches that "the way we see the problem is the problem". In a marriage that has gone flat, for example, the husband might hope that "some new book, some seminar" will improve the wife's understanding. "Or maybe... it's useless, and only a new relationship will provide the love I need." Covey urges a fresh look:

"But is it possible that my spouse isn't the real problem? Could I be empowering my spouse's weaknesses and making my life a function of the way I'm treated? Do I have some basic paradigm about my spouse, about marriage, about what love really is, that is feeding the problem?"

What does this questioning, valid or otherwise, have to do with business management? Covey bills *Seven Habits* as a "business book", so how does he make the connection? His answer is that an "inside-out" approach to personal and interpersonal effectiveness – from the inner mind and spirit to external relationships – applies in both public and private aspects of life. Indeed, "private victories precede public victories." Covey postulates a Win/Win trade-off: if you want to have more freedom, more latitude in your job, you win them by a private victory – "be a more responsible, more helpful, and more contributing employee".

The Seven Habits have a crucial role in forming the bridge between private victory and public victory: or between the Character Ethic and effectiveness. They are:

- Be Proactive
- Begin with the End in Mind
- Put First Things First
- Think Win/Win
- Seek First to Understand... Then to be Understood
- Synergize
- Sharpen the Saw

Virtually every self-help writer, whether selling the Character Ethic or the Personality Ethic, has offered some, if not all, of these precepts. People have long been urged to

"If you want to improve in major ways – I mean dramatic, revolutionary, transforming ways – if you want to make quantum improvements, either as an individual or as an organization, change your frame of reference."
Principle-centred Leadership (1990)

take control of their destinies, to form objectives, to prioritize, to seek mutual benefits, to learn by listening, to make the whole worth more than its parts, and to exercise their talents and faculties ("sharpen the saw"). But why does Covey call these precepts "habits"?

He defines "habit" along the lines of a well-known management formula: knowing what to do, knowing how to do it, and (the difficult part) actually doing it. As Covey rewords the formula: "Knowledge is the theoretical paradigm, the *what to do* and the *why*. Skill is the *how to do*. And desire is the motivation, the *want to do*." In Covey's view, the Seven Habits accompany an all-important personal development mirroring that of the human being from a dependent infancy to independence and finally, as "we continue to grow and mature", to increasing awareness that "all of nature is *interdependent*", including human life – and business management.

Maturity continuum

Along this developmental route, the first three Habits, developed in sequence, thus achieve a private victory that takes the individual from dependence to independence. Public victory comes about through adopting, one by one, the next four Habits, which take the individual into interdependence and continued self-improvement. Covey describes this as a Maturity Continuum, for which he makes the largest possible claims:

"The Seven Habits are not a set of separate or piecemeal formulas. In harmony with the natural laws of growth, they provide an incremental, sequential, highly integrated approach to the development of personal and interpersonal effectiveness."

The large claims do not stop with that amazingly confident statement. Because the Seven Habits are based on enduring and universal principles, writes Covey, *"they bring the maximum long-term beneficial results possible"* [my italics]. If that generalization sounds implausible, Covey breaks it down into subordinate claims, more specific but no less sweeping, that present the Habits as high roads to effectiveness. They create "an empowering centre of correct maps" that show you how to solve problems and maximize opportunities. Moreover, you can "continually learn and integrate other principles in an upward spiral of growth".

Character-forming habits

These enormous benefits follow, Covey maintains, as the Seven Habits "become the basis of a person's character". In other words, prioritizing your time is not merely an example of effective behaviour, like keeping your car in good condition, but a foundation of your ethical being. He thus reverses the normal concept of character, which is that good character reveals itself in good behaviour. In Covey's view, good behaviour creates good character.

The seven particular elements of good (or rather effective) behaviour that he selects are all you need, he believes, to achieve wonderful results in practical affairs. Behave better, and you will do better. Employers thus learn to treat their employees better, in order to be met half-way by employees who want to do better work. The teaching radiates optimism. Covey firmly believes in people's ability to improve, to work together for their mutual advantage, and to sweep away the many impediments that stop organizations and those who work in them from realizing their full potential.

The P/PC balance

Covey is by no means blind to these obstacles or to their importance. But in *Seven Habits* he elevates one barrier above all others – an imbalance between Production (P) and Production Capability (PC). Here he switches his emphasis from family and self to organization and organizer. Where he normally argues from the personal to the organizational (as from parental relationships to business), in this passage he argues from business to persons.

The P/PC Balance is a well-understood, rock-solid concept that is basic to all effective management. The determining force is not ethical but economic. If you run a machine flat out, it will eventually break down and production will stop. Run the machine with time allowed for preventative maintenance, however, and you will optimize the machine's life and thus its output. The principle, like so much of management, is plain commonsense, and *Seven Habits* illustrates this eternal truth with a story from Aesop, the great Greek master of the commonsensical.

Aesop famously tells about the farmer who, blessed with a goose that lays golden eggs, kills it to get at them more quickly – and thus loses the supply for ever. Whether the assets are physical, financial, or human, Covey shows that such results-obsessed greed neglects the P/PC balance and leads to ineffectiveness – often total failure. The physical asset, the machine, may become irreparable. The financial asset, the capital with which you bought the machine, will disappear unless the machine's production earns more than the cost of that capital. Drive the human assets to achieve the highest possible output at the lowest possible employment costs, and demoralized people will frustrate your aims.

Covey's clear conclusion is that managers are wrong to measure effectiveness by results alone – by the production of golden eggs. True effectiveness, he says, is "a function of two things: what is produced and the producing asset or capacity to produce." Concentration on results can be deeply counter-productive: awful examples crop up in the financial pages every day. Companies that fall from grace often appear to have suffered some sudden calamity. In reality, they have been steadily killing the golden goose for years, by neglecting staff, or customers, or investment, or innovation – perhaps all four – while continuing to report apparently excellent profits.

Short-term success

Pressure placed on subordinate managers to produce short-term results often accompanies this debilitating process and has the same counter-productive effect. Covey illustrates the consequences well by describing a manager who is eager to make a good impression on his superiors and ramps up production, with no downtime and no maintenance. "He runs the machine day and night. The production is phenomenal, costs are down, and profits skyrocket. Within a short time, he's promoted."

The manager's successor, though, has to invest heavily to compensate for the neglected downtime and maintenance. "Costs rocket; profits nose-dive." The new person, of course, gets blamed for the loss of golden eggs: but the departed manager is the true villain who, says Covey, "liquidated the asset". The accounting system was also guilty: it "only reported unit production, costs, and profit". Without information on PC, management can look far better than it is, but only for a time. Eventually, reality asserts itself.

Covey echoes well-established research that confirms the commonsense expectation that declines in quality relative to price will result in loss of customers. The customers' regard for the value for money that they receive is the marketing equivalent of a machine's capacity to produce. Lower the value for money – Covey cites a new owner who

Optimizing production
Production Capability (PC) is enlarged in motor manufacture by the use of robots. But the robots themselves must be maintained to prevent gradual erosion of the optimum Production/PC balance.

watered down a restaurant's famous clam chowder – and you reduce your sales capability. The conduct of the cheating shopkeeper is thus bad business as well as bad ethics. Covey has made the necessary connection between Character and effectiveness.

The argument is just as strong when it comes to employees. They, Covey argues, are a vital part of the marketing equation, because they deal with the customers and therefore relate directly to sales capability. *"The PC principle is always to treat your employees exactly as you want them to treat your best customers."*

Profit in the long term

Covey does not dwell on the paradox that sacrificing profit (by spending money on employee training and welfare, say) increases profit (by raising employee and customer satisfaction and thus sales). He simply observes that immediate profit – "a short-term bottom line" – is important, "but it isn't all-important". That raises the obvious question of how and where the balance is drawn. Covey admits that there is no easy answer. Rather...

> "To maintain the P/PC Balance, the balance between the golden egg (production) and the health and welfare of the goose (production capability) is often a difficult judgement call."

His argument is that, if you constantly keep the principle of balance in mind, it serves as a "lighthouse", guiding you towards the destination of optimum effectiveness. In *The Seven Habits of Highly Effective People*, Covey calls it "the very essence of effectiveness" and declares that "We can work with it or against it, but it's there.... It's the definition and paradigm upon which the Seven Habits... are based."

Universal profits

According to Covey, anybody can become highly effective by changing their lives and lifestyles through the adoption of a few easily presented and understood principles of conduct. No matter what your genetic inheritance, no matter what your life circumstances, you can become a much better person and (by no coincidence) a much better employee and manager. He stresses that this is no quick fix, but a continuous programme of self-improvement, easy to follow, whose benefits never cease, but only increase. The input is spiritual, but the benefits are also material, and, above all, universal.

Ideas into action

- Do unto others as you would have others do unto you.

- Accept full responsibility for your own character and behaviour.

- Understand that very often the way you see the problem is the problem.

- Use the "inside-out" approach to effectiveness, advancing from private victories to public success.

- Remember that effectiveness is a function of both what is produced and the capacity to produce.

- Do not apply pressure for short-term results at the expense of long-term capability.

- Replace quick fixes with continuous self-improvement.

Finding the Character Ethic

Stephen Covey is precise about the moment when his key idea, the difference between the Personality and Character Ethics, "clicked into place". He described it as "one of those 'Aha!' experiences in human life".

Typically for Covey, the moment was rooted in a family situation. One of his sons was doing badly at school, academically, socially, and in athletics, especially baseball. Covey and his wife tried as hard as they could to encourage the boy to improve.

The example Covey gives as evidence of their encouragement is baseball, not schoolwork. "We attempted to psych him up using positive mental attitude techniques." Their over-anxious coaching failed. "Our son would cry and insist that he'd never be any good and that he didn't like baseball anyway." The parental struggle ("Nothing we did seemed to help, and we were really worried") happened to coincide with bimonthly presentations in which Covey was teaching communication and participation to IBM executives as part of their development programme.

The teaching taught him about perceptions. His work on expectancy theory and self-fulfilling prophecies led to "a realization of how deeply embedded our perceptions are". Embedded perceptions, the Coveys came to see, had influenced their attitude towards their son. "When we honestly examined our deepest feelings, we realized that our perception was that he was basically inadequate, somehow 'behind'." At this point, a third factor coincidentally came into play.

Principled ways

Covey had been engaged in an "in-depth study of the success literature published in the United States since 1776". For the first 150 years, he observed, this literature had concentrated on principles as the foundations of success – "things like integrity, humility, fidelity, temperance, courage, justice, patience, industry, simplicity, modesty, and the Golden Rule [do unto others as you would have others do unto you]". These were the qualities he was to enshrine in his Character Ethic.

For the last 50 years, though, success literature had changed radically, and not, in Covey's opinion, for the better. Much of the writing was superficial, leading to what Covey describes as the Personality Ethic: "Success became more a function of personality, of public image, of attitudes and behaviour, skills and techniques, that lubricate the processes of human interaction."

In their efforts with their son, the Coveys had been following "the basic thrust" of the latter: "quick-fix influence techniques, power strategies, communication skills, and positive attitudes". Their son's problems, in other words, lay as much with his parents as himself. The Coveys decided to adopt a basically

"... we began to see our son in terms of his own uniqueness. We saw within him layers and layers of potential that would be realized at his own pace."
The Seven Habits of Highly Effective People

sensible attitude: "We decided to relax and get out of his way and let his own personality emerge." Left to carry on "at his own pace and speed", the boy blossomed in all the areas — academic performance, social relations, and athletics — where he had previously been found wanting. For the father, this was a moment of epiphany.

2

Winning private victories

Racing to your goals via self-affirmation and visualization of success ● Using "self-awareness, imagination, conscience, and independent will" to be proactive ● **How reactive language becomes a self-fulfilling prophecy** ● Enlarging the Circle of Influence that contains what is within your control ● **The importance of making and keeping commitments and promises** ● How the "first creation" (the plan) relates to the "second creation" (the execution) ● **Writing your personal "mission statement"**

The idea of the "private victory" is indispensable to Covey's whole body of thought. His philosophy stands or falls on the proposition that man is the master of his soul and the captain of his fate. The issue is not what befalls you, but how you respond to the event – the "stimulus". In the deterministic model that Covey scorns, the response is conditioned by nature and nurture, and the individual reacts accordingly. In Covey's model, "Freedom to Choose" is the governing force.

Even when trapped physically in a Nazi concentration camp, the prisoner could *"decide within himself how all of this was going to affect him"* [Covey's italics]. The guards could humiliate and destroy the body, but they could not control the mind. By exercising that control, the victim can win a private victory that cannot be taken away. If freedom of choice can be exercised in such extreme circumstances, how much easier it is, Covey implies, to deal with the challenges of normal life. The key word in his freedom model is "proactive", defined by one dictionary as:

"... tending actively to instigate changes in anticipation of future developments, as opposed to merely reacting to events as they occur; ready to take the initiative, acting without being prompted by others."

Choosing your response

The definition contains the essence of Covey's doctrine – especially the contrast between "mere" reaction and acting on one's own initiative. In this philosophy, the individual who chooses to adopt Covey's Habit One – "Be Proactive" – brings four powerful weapons to bear: self-awareness, imagination, conscience, and independent will. All four weapons are available to anybody. The difference between the highly effective person and others is that the former consciously uses the weapons. That demonstrates responsibility, or rather "response-ability", which Covey defines as "the ability to choose your response". Highly proactive people, he argues:

"recognize that responsibility; they do not blame circumstances, conditions, or conditioning for their behaviour. Their behaviour is a product of their own conscious choice, based on values, rather than a product of their conditions, based on feeling... if our lives are a function of conditioning and conditions, it is because we have, by conscious decision or by default, chosen to empower those things to control us."

This extreme individualism comes somewhat oddly from an adherent of a rigorously prescriptive fundamentalist religion. Neither Covey nor his children chose to be born into the Mormon Church, and religions naturally do not encourage those visited by the accident of birth to make a different choice. Proactive decisions and eternal verities are contrasts, not complements. But Covey squares this circle by the three words "based on values". So, if Mormon children were able to exercise total freedom of choice, their decision would surely be to live by the Mormon faith they have been taught – consequently, no conflict arises.

"Because of our unique human endowments, we can write new programmes for ourselves totally apart from our instincts and training. This is why an animal's capacity is relatively limited and man's is unlimited." *The Seven Habits of Highly Effective People*

Being proactive, not reactive

Covey takes the argument for proactive behaviour to extremes. By arguing that people are essentially proactive, he comes near to criticizing reactive behaviour – even though it is completely natural. "When people treat [reactive people] well, they feel well," he notes, with apparent disapproval. Does enjoying others' approval really merit the criticism that reactive people "build their emotional lives around the behaviour of others, empowering the weaknesses of other people to control them"? True, becoming "defensive or protective" when criticized may justify that assertion, but the "fight or flight" reaction to attack is as basic to human nature as "smile and the world smiles with you".

Negative responses

Covey insists that "It is our willing permission, our consent to what happens to us, that hurts us, more than what happens to us in the first place." But even he admits that "this is very hard to accept emotionally". It is hard because he is asking people, not to suppress their emotional reactions, which at least is a possibility, but to stop the emotions arising in the first place.

"If we have a deep understanding of our centre and our purpose we can review and recommit to it frequently. In our daily spiritual renewal, we can visualize and 'live out' the events of the day in harmony with those values." *The Seven Habits of Highly Effective People*

The negative response to stimulus, however, may well be more powerful than the positive incentives to overcome the negatives. Covey knows this very well from experience. You can take the horse to water, but you cannot make him drink. The reaction to what Covey calls "solution selling", and describes as "a key paradigm in business success", is typical of many consultants' experience:

"Over the years I have frequently counselled people who wanted better jobs to show more initiative... to study the industry, even the specific problems the organizations they are interested in are facing, and then to develop an effective presentation showing how their abilities can solve the organization's problems.... The response is usually agreement – most people can see how powerfully such an approach would affect their opportunities for employment or advancement. But many of them fail to take the necessary steps, the initiative, to make it happen."

Taking proactive initiatives

The difference in effectiveness between those who take initiatives and those who do not is not 25–50 per cent, says Covey, but "a 5,000-plus per cent difference, particularly if they are smart, aware, and sensitive to others". The figuring may well be exaggerated – 5,000 per cent is 50 times more effective – but Covey is plainly right. If you do not take the initative, things will happen to you, but you will not make things happen (except permissively).

Proactive initiatives are taken at the personal level. For example, anyone can see the illogic of the statement "He makes me so angry". As behavioural psychologists have long taught, nobody makes you angry: you choose to react angrily to somebody's provocation. The logic is as obvious as the illogic. You, not the other person, are responsible for your anger, which you can prevent or eliminate. You know how to respond differently. You need simply to escape from reaction to proaction, as exemplified by the other changes of language given below:

Reactive Language	Proactive Language
■ He makes me so angry	■ I control my own feelings
■ There's nothing I can do	■ Let's look at alternatives
■ That's just the way I am, I can't change	■ I can choose a different approach
■ I can't	■ I choose
■ I must	■ I prefer

As Covey points out, "a serious problem with reactive language is that it becomes a self-fulfilling prophecy." If you assume that somebody will not agree to your request and do not make it, you guarantee that you will receive a refusal – you say "No" on their behalf when they might, with or without suitable persuasion, say "Yes". However, you have to accept that, even when you do take a proactive course in such circumstances, you may still not be able to control, or even influence, the final decision.

"Businesses... organizations of every kind – including families – can be proactive. They can combine the creativity and resourcefulness of proactive individuals to create a proactive culture within the organization." *The Seven Habits of Highly Effective People*

Seeking to influence

Covey observes that everybody has a "Circle of Concern", containing everything that matters to them. But "there are some things over which we have no real control and others that we can do something about." The latter can be circumscribed within a smaller "Circle of Influence". Proactive people focus their efforts in this circle and seek to enlarge it. Reactive people focus on the entire Circle of Concern and focus on the weakness of other people, the problems in the environment, and other circumstances over which they have no control.

The result is that their Circle of Influence contracts, and they become less effective. Theirs is the mirror image of another aberration in which "because of position, wealth, role, or relationships… a person's Circle of Influence is larger than his or her Circle of Concern". The autocratic boss who treats his or her people as "gofers", subject to every whim or command, is a case in point. Covey regards this "self-inflicted emotional myopia" as ineffective because it makes people purely reactive.

Covey provides an example of an underling who rose above a reactive crowd of executive "gofers" by proactively anticipating his autocratic boss's needs and exceeding his expectations. The case reads uneasily like currying favour, and Covey does say that some of the man's colleagues reacted vindictively. They were probably wrong, however, to place their boss's tyranny in the third of Covey's three categories of human problems:

■ Direct control (involving our own behaviour)
■ Indirect control (involving other people's behaviour)
■ No control (problems that we can do nothing about, such as our past or present situational realities).

The colleagues' Circle of Concern contained the following statement: "*If only I had* a boss who wasn't such a dictator." The italics are Covey's. He observes that the Circle of Concern is filled with "have's". The Circle of Influence, however, is filled with "be's": thus, "I can be a more effective executive who isn't pushed around." The hero of his anecdote, to improve his situation, worked not on his boss's weaknesses but on himself.

Covey is by no means naive, and recognizes that people can neither control all the consequences of their actions, nor avoid making mistakes — the two obviously being linked. "The proactive approach to a mistake," he writes, "is to acknowledge it instantly, correct and learn from it. This literally turns a failure into a success." Failing to observe this principle "usually puts a person on a self-deceiving, self-justifying path, often involving rationalization (rational lies) to self and others."

The proactive course of action is not to lie, but "to make and keep commitments and promises". Covey teaches as a crucial part of the Character Ethic that "As we make and keep commitments, even small commitments, we begin to establish an inner integrity that gives us the awareness of self-control and the courage and strength to accept more of the responsibility for our own lives." Reaching an objective is delivering on a commitment. The proactive person learns "to set a goal — and work to achieve it", which brings Covey to the second of his habits for private victory.

Defining the objective

Covey's Habit Two is "Begin with the End in Mind". Behavioural psychologists sometimes invite people to compose their own epitaphs or obituaries as a means of focusing on their objectives in life. Covey goes further by inviting readers to their own funerals. At that ceremony, what would you want a family member, a friend, a colleague, or a church or community member to say about you and your life? "What contributions, what achievements would you want them to remember?"

The funeral is a strong metaphor for how to "begin with the end in mind". Another Covey metaphor is the business plan, which must start with a clear definition of what you are trying to accomplish. "The extent to which you begin with the end in mind determines whether or not you are able to create a successful enterprise." Most business failures, he observes, begin when this stage of mental or "first" creation leads to problems "such as under-capitalization, misunderstanding of the market" or simply having no plan. The correct process is as follows:

> "You carefully think through the product or service you want to provide in terms of your market target, then you organize all the elements – financial, research and development, operations, marketing, personnel, physical facilities, and so on – to meet that objective."

Personal mission statements

The business plan, or "first creation" in Covey's terms, is followed by the "second creation", which is putting the plan into practice. Covey makes the telling point that "there is a first creation to every part of our lives". The issue is whether people work to their "own proactive design", or "are the second creation of other people's agendas, of circumstances, or of past habits". To become your own first creator, according to Covey, requires considerable imagination and conscience. Combining these with self-awareness "empowers us to write our own script" – in other words, to write our own "personal mission statement".

The concept is familiar to the corporate world, where vision and mission statements try, usually with some difficulty, to follow Covey's recipe. The statement "focuses on what you want to be... and to do... and on the values or principles upon which being and doing are based." The difficulty for corporations is that their statements end up sounding much alike. Individuals, too, are likely to subscribe to similar values – that, after all, is one of Covey's basic tenets: thus few people would disagree with one of Covey's friends who recommends "Keep a sense of humour" or "Be orderly in person and in work".

It follows that preparing your personal mission statement must be taken very seriously. Covey expects "deep introspection, careful analysis, thoughtful expression, and often many rewrites." As with the corporate equivalent, "the process is as important as the product". Writing a statement or reviewing it (which Covey personally does "fairly regularly") changes you "because it forces you to think through your priorities deeply, carefully, and to align your behaviour with your beliefs."

Visualizing and affirming

Making the statement brings into play the right side of the brain, where intuition and creativity are primarily located. Covey observes that ours is "a primarily left brain-dominated world, where words and logic are enthroned." He is apparently not an expert in brain function, since he seems unaware that women are much less likely to be dominated by the left hemisphere. But that does not affect his main point, which is that imagination or visualization (both right-brain functions) are important ways of changing and improving how you perform.

"Before a performance, a sales presentation, a difficult confrontation, or the daily challenge of meeting a goal, see it clearly, vividly, relentlessly, over and over again. Create an internal 'comfort zone'. Then, when you get into the situation, it isn't foreign. It doesn't scare you."

Visualization is accompanied in Covey's philosophy by "*affirmation*". By that he means a personal statement that keeps your vision and values before you and aligns your life to be "congruent with those most important things". A good affirmation has five basic ingredients: it is personal; it is positive; it is present tense; it is visual; and it is emotional.

Drawing an illustration of visualization from carefully considered domestic life, Covey cites a parental statement that "It is deeply satisfying that I respond with wisdom, love, firmness, and self-control when my children misbehave." Having made the statement, you visualize the situation – a child misbehaving badly in this case – and visualize your proactive response. Repeating this process day after day will, he teaches, change your behaviour until you are "living out of the script" that you have written from your own "self-selected value system".

"You will find that there is enormous power in the principle of keeping promises and honouring commitments. It leads to strong self-esteem and personal integrity, the foundation of all true success." *Principle-centred Leadership*

Committing to goals

Covey often talks of life management in stage terms (such as "script"). He also recommends that you break down your mission statement into the "specific role areas of your life" (maybe acting as salesperson, manager, or product developer in your business role). You then decide on "the goals you want to accomplish in each area". Goal-setting is again a right-brain function, which "uses imagination, creativity, conscience, and inspiration", and which focuses "primarily on results rather than activity". Covey argues that simply identifying the various areas of your life and the two or three important results you wish to achieve "gives you an overall perspective of your life and a sense of direction".

Covey believes that mission statements should not only be drawn up by organizations, but also by families (his own puts the statement on a wall and reviews it frequently). In both these cases, involvement of everybody is crucial. In fact, Covey gives this principle extraordinary emphasis: "Without involvement there is no commitment. Mark it down, asterix it, circle it, underline it. *No involvement, no commitment* [his italics]."

Managing yourself

Achieving "personal victory", by which you turn your vision into reality by proactive, purposeful self-control, and thus escape from dependence into independence, requires a third Habit. Habit Three – "Put First Things First" – is the "fulfilment, the actualization, the natural emergence of Habits One and Two" [to wit, "Be Proactive" and "Begin with the End in Mind"]. Those who acquire the Third Habit become "principle-centred day-in and day-out" by living the habit and "practising effective self-management". This Habit is not theoretical: it is a practical programme. The Franklin Day Planner, a bestselling time organizer that today brings in large profits for Covey's company, was inspired by Habit Three.

Covey's approach (see also Masterclass 3, on p. 88), is based around a Time Management Matrix, which divides activities into the four "quadrants" outlined below. Covey emphasizes that "Time Management" is "really a misnomer – the challenge is not to manage time, but to manage ourselves... Rather than focusing on things and time... focus on preserving and enhancing relationships and on accomplishing results – in short, on maintaining the P/PC Balance [see p. 21]."

TIME-MANAGEMENT MATRIX

	Urgent	Not Urgent

Important	Crises
	Pressing problems
	Deadline-driven
	   projects
		Prevention, PC activities
		Relationship building
		Recognizing new
		   opportunities
		Planning, recreation

Not Important	Interruptions, calls Some mail, reports Some meetings Proximate, pressing matters Popular activities	Trivia, busy work Some mail Some phone calls Time wasters Pleasant activities

People who focus on the problems in Quadrant I can look forward, says Covey, to stress and burnout as they forever put out fires and practise "crisis management". Those locked in Quadrant III, focusing on "things that are urgent, assuming that they are also important", also suffer the pains of crisis management, along with short-termism, shallow or broken relationships, and a reputation for having a "chameleon character". Quadrant III inhabitants see goals and plans as worthless, and feel victimized, out of control. As for those "who spend time almost exclusively in Quadrants III and IV," they "basically lead irresponsible lives," asserts Covey, being dependent on others or on institutions for basic support. They are in total contrast to the Quadrant II dwellers, who, spending most of their time on important but not urgent matters, show vision and perspective, balance, discipline and control, and suffer few crises.

Managing through delegation

But effective personal management paradoxically involves others. "We accomplish all that we do", writes Covey, "through delegation – either to time or to other people. If we delegate to time [allocating it to the purpose concerned], we think efficiency. If we delegate to other people, we think effectiveness."

Covey argues that effective delegation, which he calls "stewardship", gives people a choice of method and makes them, and not the delegator, responsible for results. The key is to secure "clear, up-front, mutual understanding and commitment regarding expectations in five areas":

■ Desired results: agree on what needs to be accomplished, focusing on what, not how.

- Guidelines: identify the parameters within which the delegate should operate – as few as possible.
- Resources: identify the human, technical, financial, or organizational resources available.
- Accountability: establish the standards that will be applied, and when reporting and evaluation will take place.
- Consequences: specify what will happen, both good and bad, as a result of the evaluation.

The formula is basic to Covey's theories of business management. It is the bridge between the personal victory and the public achievement that springs from that success.

Ideas into action

- Demonstrate "response-ability", or the ability to choose your response.

- Do not wait for something to happen or someone to take care of you.

- Combat bad times by adopting practical, do-able counter-measures.

- Do not waste time over matters you can do nothing about.

- Acknowledge mistakes instantly, correct them, and learn from them.

- Always start new ventures with a clear vision of your goal in mind.

- Think through your priorities carefully and align your behaviour with your beliefs.

Choosing the response to stimulus

One year, Stephen Covey took a writing sabbatical from his university job, living near a college in Laie (right) on the Hawaiian island of Oahu. A passage in a book (which he does not identify) caught his attention.

Covey writes: "My eyes fell upon a single paragraph that powerfully influenced the rest of my life." It contained a short phrase that "hit me with fresh, almost unbelievable force". The words seem quite ordinary – "a gap between stimulus and response". But they immediately suggested a simple idea of great appeal to Covey: that the key to human growth and happiness is how people choose to use that space between stimulus and response.

He "can hardly describe the effect that idea had on my mind." Since he had been "nurtured in the philosophy of self-determination", the force of this revelation is perhaps surprising. The impact lay less in the novelty of the idea than in that very force. It jolted Covey outside his existing paradigm:

> "It was as if I had become an observer of my own participation. I began to stand in that gap and to look outside at the stimuli. I revelled in the inward

sense of freedom to choose my response – even to become the stimulus, or at least to influence it, even to reverse it."

Covey followed up his revelation by beginning a prolonged practice of "deep communication" with his wife, Sandra. He called for her just before noon every day, and they cycled out to a secluded beach with their two pre-school children, picnicked, and talked, going deeper and deeper into their "internal worlds... our upbringing, our scripting, our feelings, and self-doubts".

Inner exploration

The couple "began to use that space between stimulus and response... to think about how we were programmed and how these programs shaped how we saw the world." The experience involved some pain as we "unfolded the inner layers of vulnerability" – though the example Covey gives is certainly odd. Sandra "seemed to have an

obsession about Frigidaire appliances that I was at an absolute loss to understand."

The obsession is no odder than the fact that it became "a matter of considerable agitation to me". Both slightly manic afflictions were cured when the probing revealed that Sandra's obsession sprang from her deep relationship with her father, whose business had been saved when the Frigidaire company financed his inventory.

What Covey and his wife had discovered in that "wonderful year" of mutual psychological exploration was that the "outside-in" approach was ultimately ineffective. When the couple began to "work from the

"It takes courage to realize that you are greater than your moods, greater than your thoughts, and that you can control your moods and thoughts."
First Things First

---

inside out, we were able… to resolve dysfunctional differences in a deep and lasting way".

Covey had defined the underpinning idea of his multi-million bestseller: that working on their essential paradigms, people have the ability to centre their lives on correct principles "and become empowered in the task of creating effective, useful, and peaceful lives".

Exercising self-leadership

*L*eading and influencing other people require first that you take control of yourself, in the positive sense of making the most of your abilities and opportunities. To achieve this, you must learn to think proactively and to take the initiative whenever possible. You must also set your own short and long-term goals and develop your capability to achieve them.

STEPHEN COVEY

Use self-awareness

Stephen Covey regards self-awareness, the ability to think about your own thought processes, as a unique human ability and the secret of human success. It is the first of four keys to freedom of choice between reactive behaviour (being controlled by others) and proactive behaviour (taking control of yourself).

Start to take control of your life by practising active self-awareness. Do the following self-awareness assessment. Can you answer "Yes" to the first five questions and "No" to the last?

■ Can you view yourself as though you were someone else?
■ Can you identify your present mood?
■ Can you name what you are feeling?
■ Can you describe your present mental state?
■ Is your mind working quickly and alertly?
■ Are you torn between doing this exercise and evaluating the point to be made from it? The point is, if you answer "No" to the questions, practise until you can answer "Yes".

The proactive course

According to Covey, the other three keys to proactive behaviour are: conscience (a sense of right and wrong); independent will (the readiness to act on your own, as your self-awareness dictates); and imagination (the use of the creative, right-hand side of the brain).

By exercising and developing all four abilities, you can become a more effective human being, gaining the power to be and do what *you* want, not just what others want from you. By winning this freedom of choice you empower yourself to take control of your own destiny and fulfil your potential. This masterclass shows you ways of improving all four of Covey's key abilities.

1 Watching your words

The language you use is a strong indicator of whether you are merely reacting to events or proactively influencing them. Adopt proactive language to bring a positive transformation in how you view yourself and in how others respond to you.

Self-limiting language

The principle is simple. If you do not enter a race, you cannot win. Covey's argument, a very true one, is that people under-perform because they consciously or unconsciously limit their ambitions. They show this self-limitation by their language. Analyze your own language to see how much you hold yourself back in the way you express yourself. For every self-limiting, or reactive, phrase there is a proactive equivalent that puts you in the driving seat.

Reactive and Proactive Language	
Reactive Language	**Proactive Language**
There's no point in asking my boss, he'll only say "No".	I'll make him an offer he won't be able to refuse.
I couldn't do that, it's not my sort of thing.	I've never done that before, but I'd love to try.
I've got no head for figures and making mental calculations.	I'm going to work hard to improve my numeracy.

Use positive language

Concentrate for a full day, advises Covey, on listening to your own language and that of others. Ask yourself, how often do I use and hear reactive phrases such as "If only", "I must", or "I have to"? You will almost certainly be surprised at the frequency.

From then on, whenever you find a reactive phrase coming to your lips, turn it around to the proactive opposite. For example, replace "If only" with "I will", "I must" with "I prefer", and "I have to" with "I will choose". The shift will work to reverse any unconscious passivity in your attitude and can dramatically change your behaviour and raise your effectiveness.

2 Taking the initiative

You can take control of your destiny. That most people do not, says Covey, is contrary to proactive human nature. Do not empower conditions and conditioning to run your life. Empower yourself by your behaviour and by widening your influence over events.

Develop proactive behaviour

Covey suggests that you check how proactive you are by using a programme that demonstrates your responsibility for your own effectiveness. For a period of 30 days, try to adhere to the following seven instructions in all your activities, at work and in the home:

- Make small commitments and keep them.
- Be part of the solution, not part of the problem.
- Be a model, not a critic.
- When you make a mistake, admit it, correct it, and learn from it – immediately.
- Do not blame and accuse.
- If you start to think the problem is "out there", and not your responsibility, stop yourself.

At the end of each day, write down how you have performed on each of the seven instructions. Keep the instructions in the forefront of your mind and aim to improve every day.

Use your imagination

Encourage yourself to take the initiative by using visual "affirmations", which might be called purposeful day-dreaming. A successful afffirmation contains five distinctive elements.

The Five Elements of Visual Affirmation
It is personal.
It is positive.
It is present tense.
It is emotional.
It is visual.

STEPHEN COVEY

For example, faced with a senseless decision from your superior that
you do not wish to carry out, use a visual affirmation to help you
take the proactive course – persuading your boss to change his or her
mind. Your affirmation might be: "I get a real high (emotional)
because I (personal) respond (present tense) with honesty, courage,
and self-control (positive) to stop mistakes being made." Then
visualize yourself entering your boss's office and convincing him or
her. Next, do it – and do not be surprised when it works.

Widen your circle of influence

There are some matters over which you have control, and others
that concern you, but where you can do nothing. They all belong in
what Covey calls the Circle of Concern. Those you can affect are
directly in the core, the Circle of Influence.

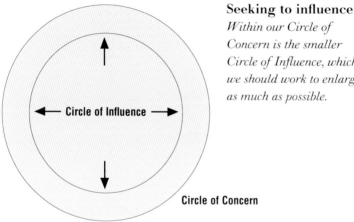

Seeking to influence
*Within our Circle of
Concern is the smaller
Circle of Influence, which
we should work to enlarge
as much as possible.*

Use your initiative to widen your Circle of Influence, and use your
self-control to concentrate your time and energy on issues you can
affect. When you face a problem, always ask:
- Is this something over which I have no control?
- Is this something over which I have direct control?
- Is this something over which I have indirect control?
If the answer is (1), learn to live with the difficulty. If the answer is
(2), use your powers to resolve the issue. If the answer is (3), use
your powers to influence people in the direction you want.

3 Setting your goals

Identify where you want to go and how you are going to get there.
Doing so is fundamental to taking control of yourself. Without a
clear objective, you will miss the signposts that show you the way.
As Louis Pasteur observed, "Fortune favours the prepared mind."

Decide your mission

Write down your chief ambition in a mission statement. Make it
short and to the point. For example, "To be chief executive of a
major publicly quoted company by the age of 40." Just deciding on
that prime objective is a major step towards achieving it.

You can now focus all your other activities and lesser objectives
towards that end. You will then start to notice events, opportunities,
material, and contacts (the signposts) that will help you attain your
prime objective. Putting a time to the target is very important in
disciplining and directing your efforts – and you may well find that
the objective is reached earlier than you thought possible.

Plan strategically

Naming your prime objective is only the start. You are engaged in
personal strategic planning, and need to follow the same procedure
as a corporate planner. That involves answering these questions:

- Where am I now (position A)?
- Where do I want to be, and when (position B)?
- What resources are required to get from A to B?
- Which do I possess now?
- What development do those resources need?
- What other required resources must I find?
- How can I find them?
- What stages must I pass before reaching the final
  objective – and when?
- What help will I need, and from whom?

Covey describes this process as mental creation. Begin by applying it
to a project that you will be undertaking in the near future. Write
down the results you desire and the steps that will lead to those
results. Success in smaller projects will build your confidence in the
planning of your long-term personal mission.

STEPHEN COVEY

4 Optimizing your capability

Effectiveness does not operate in the single dimension of the work you get through and how excellently it is done. You must also nurture and enhance your capacity to perform, your Production Capability (PC), if you are to make the most of your abilities.

Develop capability

The more knowledge you have, the greater your ambition, and the more and better the components of your skills-set, the more effective you will be. The Seven Habits all provide critical elements of PC, which needs to be developed in just the same way as athletes build body power (their form of PC) – by training and exercise.

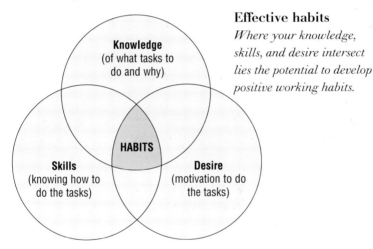

Knowledge
(of what tasks to do and why)

HABITS

Skills
(knowing how to do the tasks)

Desire
(motivation to do the tasks)

Effective habits
Where your knowledge, skills, and desire intersect lies the potential to develop positive working habits.

Conduct regular audits of your personal PC development and that of your organization to identify weak spots where more could be done to improve capability and thus performance. Are you acting to:
- Exert control over your destiny?
- Form valuable objectives?
- Prioritize the use of your time?
- Work with others for your mutual benefit?
- Learn by listening?
- Coordinate your work with that of others?
- Improve your physical, human, and financial resources?

3

From private to public victories

How abundance thinkers believe that "the pie is big enough for everyone to have a slice" ● Five key areas for achieving effectiveness by delegating to others ● **The four-steps that achieve "Win/Win" solutions** ● Empathetic listening as the key to making deposits in the "Emotional Bank Account" ● **Gaining influence over others by letting yourself be influenced** ● Why synergistic cooperation is essential to deal with the ambiguity of creativity ● **The four dimensions of personal renewal**

The first step from independence to interdependence, and thus towards Public Victory, is Habit Four: "Think Win/Win". Delegation (related to Habit Three: "Put First Things First") leads to the happy outcome sought through adopting Habit Four. Successful delegation means that the delegator wins, because he or she has accomplished more than could have been achieved unaided: while the delegate wins the psychic and material rewards of that success. Covey describes Win/Win as a total philosophy of human interaction. It is one of six possible paradigms:

- Win/Lose: the authoritarian ("I get my way, you don't get yours") and competitive approach ("Life is a zero sum game where some win and some lose"). This is the dominant mode, encouraged by childhood rivalry, athletics, adversarial trials in law, etc.
- Lose/Win: giving in or giving up. In leadership, "it's permissiveness or indulgence. Lose/Win means being a nice guy, even if 'nice guys finish last'."
- Lose/Lose: becoming centred on an enemy, wanting them to lose at any price. This is also the philosophy of the highly dependent person.
- Win: what matters is that you get what you want, irrespective of the effect on others.
- Win/Win or No Deal: if you cannot agree on a mutually beneficial solution, you agree to disagree, and go your separate ways.
- Win/Win: all parties feel good about the decision and committed to the action plan.

Covey's overwhelming preference for the last course does not exclude him from recognizing that other paradigms may at certain times be the most effective. Win/Lose has to be the correct approach in sports. Lose/Win is appropriate if "the expense of time and effort to achieve a win... just isn't worth it". But Covey argues that: "Most of life is an interdependent, not an independent, reality. Most results you want depend on cooperation between you and others." In that context, Win/Lose is dysfunctional – as many executives, managers, and parents find out.

They consequently "swing back and forth, as if on a pendulum, from Win/Lose inconsideration to Lose/Win indulgence" – and then back again. Win/Lose is also inappropriate when "two determined, stubborn, ego-invested individuals interact... both will lose." Even if a Win/Lose approach appears to win – if a supplier exacts an onerous deal from a customer, say – it may prove to be a long-term Lose if repeat business is jettisoned. His analysis leads Covey to a highly predictable conclusion: "Most situations... are part of an interdependent reality, and then Win/Win is really the only viable alternative."

Character and Win/Win

Win/Win has five dimensions, according to Covey:
"It begins with character and moves towards relationships, out of which flow agreements. It is nurtured in an environment where structure and systems are based on Win/Win. And it involves process; we cannot achieve Win/Win ends with Win/Lose or Lose/Win means."

Character, "the foundation of Win/Win", has three essential traits: integrity, maturity, and "abundance mentality". Covey defines integrity as "the value we place on ourselves" and maturity as "the balance between courage and consideration" (equating with the "I'm OK, you're OK" attitude of the psychological theory known as transactional analysis). "If I'm high on courage, and low on consideration," asks Covey, "how will I think? Win/Lose." Those who are low on courage and high on consideration, on the other hand, are trapped in Lose/Win. But with the high-high balance, you can listen and empathetically understand, but you can also "courageously confront".

The abundance mentality (see p. 80 for its key role in leadership) contrasts with the scarcity mentality, which sees life as "having only so much, as though there were only one pie out there", so that a bigger slice for one person means less for another. Abundance thinkers hold that there is "plenty out there and enough to spare for anybody". They are therefore in a much stronger position to reach the agreements that flow from good relationships and good communication.

The Win/Win environment

Covey is emphatic that Win/Win agreements will not work "in an environment of competition and contests". All an organization's systems have to support Win/Win; training, planning, communication, budgeting, information – and compensation. Many reward systems, notably for salespeople, are highly competitive, with winners taking home very big bonuses and losers sometimes even losing their jobs. Covey reports a case where a company switched from Win/Lose, with only 5 per cent of the sales force getting the management's awards for top performance, to self-selected individual and team objectives. After the change, four-fifths received awards – and almost all of the 800 "winners" matched the individual performances of the previous year's top 40 high-achievers.

Win/Win in four steps

You can only gain such Win/Win solutions, says Covey, with Win/Win processes – "the ends and the means are the same". He suggests a universal four-step process:

■ See the problem from the other point of view.
■ Identify the key issues and concerns involved.
■ Determine what results would constitute a fully acceptable solution.
■ Identify possible new options to achieve those results.

This process leads straight into the next two Habits, Five and Six, with which it overlaps: "Seek First to Understand... Then to be Understood" and "Synergize". Covey calls Habit Five "empathetic communication". As so often with his work, the lesson is not new. People who want to improve their communication skills have always been urged to become better listeners. But he argues that comparatively few people have actually had any training in how to listen, let alone how to "really, deeply understand another human being from that individual's own frame of reference".

Most people, as he notes, "do not listen with the intent to understand; they listen with the intent to reply. They're either speaking or preparing to speak. They're filtering

"Synergy is exciting.... It's phenomenal what openness and communication can produce. The possibilities of truly significant gain, of significant improvement are so real that it's worth the risk such openness entails." *The Seven Habits of Highly Effective People*

everything through their own paradigms." People who say they are listening may be ignoring, pretending to listen by nodding, etc, listening selectively, or being attentive, all of which fall far short of listening empathetically. Empathy is not sympathy, or even understanding the words used. "You listen for feeling, for meaning. You listen for behaviour. You use your right brain as well as your left."

Empathetic listening

Covey regards empathetic listening as "the key to making deposits in Emotional Bank Accounts". The latter are among his key concepts. They are "a metaphor that describes the amount of trust that's been built up in a relationship.... If I make deposits into an Emotional Bank Account with you through courtesy, kindness, honesty, and keeping my commitments to you, I build up a reserve." That trust can be built higher by six suggested steps:

- Understand the individual.
- Attend to the little things.
- Keep commitments.
- Clarify expectations.
- Show personal integrity.
- Apologize when you make a "withdrawal".

The apologies must be sincere: "repeated apologies interpreted as insincere make withdrawals". While the reserve is there to be drawn upon, there is a limit to the amount that can be taken out; "if I have a habit of showing discourtesy, disrespect, cutting you off, overreacting, ignoring you, becoming arbitrary, betraying your trust, threatening you, or playing little tin god in your life, eventually my Emotional Bank Account is overdrawn." But empathetic listening is, in and of itself, says Covey, "a tremendous deposit in the Emotional Bank Account".

It is also a great help in reaching the right solutions. But in contrast to the "selfless", impersonal listening of a trained doctor, most people listen "autobiographically", relating what they hear to their own experience and filtering it through that experience. According to Covey, people tend to respond in one of four ways:

Listening without prejudice

Doctors are trained to listen impersonally to information from their patients before making a diagnosis. Managers benefit enormously when they apply the same technique in their work.

- They evaluate – either agreeing or disagreeing.
- They probe – asking questions that come from their own frame of reference.
- They advise – giving counsel based on their own experience.
- They interpret – trying to "figure out" people, to explain their motives and behaviour, based on their own motives and behaviour.

Covey's generalizations here are too sweeping. People commonly question, advise, and interpret with open minds as well as closed ones, and they also refer to others' experience as well as their own.

Developing empathy

Covey takes listening through four developmental stages. You mimic content by simply repeating what the other person has said. It is slightly more effective to rephrase what you have heard ("School is for the birds!" – "You don't want to go to school any more"). You go further when you reflect feeling ("You're feeling really frustrated"). Covey claims that the fourth stage, when you both rephrase and reflect feeling ("You're feeling really frustrated about

---

"Empathetic listening gets inside another person's frame of reference. You look out through it, you see the way they see the world, you understand their paradigm, you understand how they feel." *The Seven Habits of Highly Effective People*

school"), has "really incredible" results — "the barrier between what's going on inside him and what's actually being communicated to you disappears".

In reaching that Win/Win solution, though, the other half of Habit Five, knowing how to be understood, is equally critical. Covey uses early Greek philosophy to construct a sequential three-word model: ethos (your personal credibility), pathos (empathy, your alignment with another's emotional thrust), and logos (reasoning). "Most people go straight to the logos, the left-brain logic of their ideas." You will convince others more effectively, Covey suggests, if you first put ethos, and next pathos, into consideration – and then present your logical argument.

Influencing others

He points out that many factors in interdependent situations are in your "Circle of Concern" – problems, disagreements, circumstances, and the behaviour of other people (see p. 35). These factors are outside your control. Understanding, however, is within your "Circle of Influence", or control. Moreover, because "you really listen, you become influenceable. And being influenceable is the key to influencing others." Covey therefore rightly advises setting up one-to-one time with employees, together with systems that generate "honest, accurate feedback at every level: from customers, suppliers, and employees".

Deep mutual understanding, he says, means that differences, instead of being stumbling blocks to communication and progress, become the stepping stones to winning synergy – Habit Six. Covey does not use "synergy" in any special sense. He defines it simply as meaning that the whole is worth more than the sum of its parts. The relationship between the parts, however, is itself a part, and one that rouses Covey to extreme enthusiasm: "the most catalytic, the most empowering, the most unifying, and the most exciting part".

The synergy that so arouses him is that between people, especially when they collaborate to achieve creative results. Although much of Covey's teaching could be said to encourage new ideas, creativity as such is not featured in the Seven Habits. But he regards synergistic cooperation as essential to deal with the sheer untidiness of creation.

"Most all creative endeavours are somewhat unpredictable. They often seem ambiguous, hit-or-miss, trial and error. And unless people have a high tolerance for ambiguity and get their security from integrity to principles and inner values they find it unnerving and unpleasant to be involved in highly creative enterprises. Their need for structure, certainty, and predictability is too high."

Synergistic interaction

The linkage Covey establishes between this accurate diagnosis and synergy is, by his own standards, vague and short on usable content. He says, somewhat loosely, that: "As I think back on many consultative and executive education experiences, I can say that the highlights were almost always synergistic." As such experiences by definition involve several people, that is not surprising. Whether, as people interact synergistically, "whole new worlds of insights... are opened up and thought about" is much less certain. So, it may be argued, is Covey's statement that these new ideas "usually come to some kind of closure that is practical and useful".

Covey does quote one business example that is close to his heart. He uses words like "empathetic... courageous... exciting" to describe the "synergistic process" that led to the creation of his own company's mission statement – a process that "engraved it in the hearts and minds of everyone there". This is the result:

"Our mission is to empower people and organizations to significantly increase their performance capability in order to achieve worthwhile purposes through understanding and living principle-centred leadership."

Despite Covey's pride in its creation, that statement reads as if it were written by a committee, which perhaps it was. There are times, as every manager knows, when two and two make three, not five. Covey is so enthusiastic about the enormous potential of synergy ("the crowning achievement of all the previous habits") that he glosses over the fact that it may not come naturally, and forgets, too, that generating successful alternatives need not be synergistic. He is, however, correct in saying that there are nearly always alternatives – and it is also true that two or more heads are generally better than one.

Regular self-renewal

Habit Seven, "Sharpen the Saw", surrounds "Synergize" and all the other habits "because it is the habit that makes all the others possible". The phrase comes from the man who takes an inordinately long time to saw a log because he is too busy sawing to sharpen the saw. It makes Covey's point that "balanced self-renewal" is essential for "preserving and enhancing the greatest asset you have – you". Self-renewal has four dimensions:

- Physical: eating the right kinds of foods, getting sufficient rest and relaxation, and taking adequate exercise on a regular basis.
- Spiritual: clarifying values and commitment, studying and meditating, to provide "leadership for your life".
- Mental: reading, visualizing, planning, and writing (and watching relatively little television).
- Social/emotional: centering on the principles of interpersonal leadership, empathetic communication, and creative cooperation.

Daily private victories

Covey warns that to "neglect any one area negatively impacts the rest", both for organizations and individuals. "Things you do in any one dimension have positive impact in other dimensions because they are so highly interrelated." As the key to the integrated development of the Seven Habits, he advocates the Daily Private Victory – "a minimum of one hour a day in renewal of the physical, spiritual, and mental dimensions". Covey asserts that renewal is "the principle – and the process – that empowers us to move on an upward spiral of growth and change, of continuous improvement."

"Your economic security does not lie in your job; it lies in your own power to produce – to think, to learn, to create, to adapt. That's true financial independence. It's not having wealth; it's having the power to produce wealth." *The Seven Habits of Highly Effective People*

"Growth", "change", and "continuous improvement", of course, are vital parts of modern management language, essential to the ambitions of any progressive organization. Covey's teaching suggests that the *Seven Habits* philosophy, applied to themselves by members of an organization, will transform its performance. That, however, will not happen without leadership – the theme that, developed in later writings, has generated Covey's most significant contributions to management theory and practice.

Ideas into action

■ Focus your attention first of all on relationships, rather than things or time.

■ Make delegates fully responsible for achieving their results in their own way.

■ Ensure that everybody knows the plan and feels good about it.

■ Always strive to see a situation from the other person's point of view.

■ If you need to apologize to anybody, do so immediately and sincerely.

■ Get people on your side emotionally before presenting your logical case.

■ Set aside time for regular activities that contribute to your personal improvement.

Working with other people

Interpersonal relationships are the defining medium of management. How you relate to superiors, colleagues, and subordinates governs your ability to succeed – and often theirs as well. The desire to serve mutual interests, good communication techniques, and the appreciation of opposing views result in increased trust and synergistic teamwork.

Establish good relations

Internal relationships need to be fostered just as carefully as the decisive connections outside the firm. Treat everyone you relate to – suppliers, bosses, peers, and other employees – in the same way you treat external customers; as people with specific (if unexpressed) demands, which they expect you to serve. Some companies identify the internal customers of departments and carry out customer satisfaction surveys, on the same lines as those conducted externally, to help appraise a particular department's effectiveness. It can then correct any faults that have been identified.

Satisfy all parties

The most desirable outcome with any customer – inside or outside the company – is benefit to both parties. Your object with an external customer is to give perceived value. Pursue that aim just as vigorously inside the organization. Adopt the six-stage cycle of customer satisfaction with each relevant individual or group.

The Six-Stage Cycle of Customer Satisfaction
1 Discover customer wants by asking the customers.
2 Find out how well you are currently supplying the wants.
3 Take decisive action to eliminate deficiencies.
4 Identify and install added customer value.
5 Re-check customer satisfaction.
6 Repeat stages 2–5 and continue the cycle.

STEPHEN COVEY

1 Serving mutual interests

The barriers to finding mutually acceptable and beneficial solutions are very often emotional. Hold both yourself and the other party in high esteem, act accordingly, and you greatly improve your prospect of achieving a mutually satisfactory result in any negotiation.

Encourage emotional security

Covey describes a satisfactory result for both parties as Win/Win, which equates to the top level of emotional security ("I'm OK, You're OK") described by the school of psychology called transactional analysis (TA). He identifies three other common outcomes to any negotiation. You must be high on both personal courage and consideration for others to effect a Win/Win outcome.

	Low Courage	High Courage
High Consideration	Lose/Win	Win/Win
Low Consideration	Lose/Lose	Win/Lose

Achieving Win/Win

As this matrix shows, both sides in a negotiation must display a high level of courage and consideration to achieve a Win/Win outcome.

Performance agreements

Win/Win is essential to the success of any performance agreements created by manager and subordinate (see p. 54). To form a Win/Win agreement, follow Covey's four-step action plan.

The Four-Step Action Plan to Win/Win
1 Establish what the other person's interests really are.
2 Identify the key issues and concerns involved.
3 Determine what results both sides would accept.
4 Find possible new options to achieve those results.

2 Mastering communications

Effective communications depend mainly on trust. Learn how to establish and sustain trust by avoiding hidden agendas and ill-considered actions. Focus also on developing your ability to handle disagreement, listen empathetically, and be understood yourself.

The importance of trust

Covey makes the important point that trust must be built over time, and that its level will rise and fall as different experiences have different effects. The greater the trust between two parties, the greater the degree of cooperation.

STEPHEN COVEY

Towards synergy

This matrix demonstrates how synergy occurs when all parties show high trust and cooperation.

Establish trust

Full trust is never easily achieved. But it can be earned. To make effective the time and effort spent on creating, enhancing, and restoring trust, you must abide by the golden rule: "Do unto others as you would have others do unto you." Therefore:

■ Do not "give a dog a bad name". If you treat individuals as incompetent, you will get incompetence. Treat them as competent, encourage what they do well, and they will excel.

■ Do not make a promise that you cannot keep. If you are forced to dash an individual's hopes, apologize and make amends at the first opportunity. Their trust will be hard to recapture.

■ Do not disappoint expectations. Remember that expectations can only be fulfilled by actions. To quote Covey: "Honesty is telling the truth…conforming our words to reality." Integrity is "conforming reality to our words".

Face up to disagreement

At times your message will be met by disagreement or even outright confrontation. Sometimes a subordinate will say that they agree when in fact they do not, resulting in only half-hearted cooperation, if that. To deal with such situations you need to master four essential communication skills.

The Four Essential Communication Skills
1 The ability to put yourself in the other person's shoes.
2 The ability to communicate your understanding of the opposing view.
3 The ability to listen carefully.
4 The ability to interpret the meaning of body and facial language.

Use empathy

The first two skills are different aspects of empathy. Ask yourself why the other person is thinking and acting in a contrary manner. By understanding their reasoning, and the underlying emotions, you can rescue communication from failure, and even strengthen it.

To demonstrate your understanding, play back to the other party their own view in an empathetic way, putting their case as strongly and accurately as you can. Then present your case from their point of view. Now ask the other party to explain your position as best *they* can. This will lead to better understanding on both sides and to a greater chance of reaching agreement.

Seek the full meaning

Be very sure to listen carefully. People commonly start thinking about their reply well before the other party has finished speaking. Hear the other person out. Watch them intently, too. Facial gestures and body language often contradict the words. If so, it will be the accompanying words that are misleading.

Try watching somebody talking on television with the sound turned off, while you record the programme. What do the person's gestures communicate? Now rerun the programme with the sound on, and check your analysis. How misleading are the words?

3 Winning synergy's rewards

The most effective solutions to issues are often achieved by group effort. Organize brainstorming sessions to promote the discussion of ideas, the interchange of views, and the exploration of alternatives so as to achieve synergistic agreement on the best way forward.

Using the dialectic

To bring about synergy, use the dialectic of philosophy – ensure that opposing views are aired, and that individuals are committed to finding a satisfactory solution for the group.

Dialectical Synergy		
I put forward a thesis.	You propose the antithesis.	We agree on a combined synthesis.

Debating in a force field

The conflict between positive and negative forces is as natural and as essential to synergy as the opposition of views. When you are debating an issue, you will find yourself in a force field, in which driving forces are opposed to restraining forces.

Opposing Forces in Debate	
Driving Forces	**Restraining Forces**
Positive Thought	Negative Thought
Reason	Emotion
Logic	Illogic
Consciousness	Unconsciousness
Economics	Social Factors

You will find that trying to strengthen the driving forces is not enough. So long as the restraining forces are there, they will push back, and the harder you drive, the harder they will push. But take a Win/Win attitude; try to understand the opposing point of view, and make sure you are understood yourself. Then a constructive interaction will take place – and synergy will be achieved.

STEPHEN COVEY

Two-brained thinking

Synergy sessions require the use of both sides of your brain. The division is similar to the opposition of driving and restraining forces (see p. 70). The analytical, logical, verbal left brain – which is full of driving forces – does not generate the creative, contrarian, exciting ideas. You generate these in the emotional right brain, which is intuitive, creative, and visual.

Your left brain provides the framework and the facts. The right brain provides the insight and inspiration. As Covey points out, getting the two sides of the brain to work together is synergy in itself – psychic synergy.

Group synergy sessions

To achieve two-brained working in a group, first ask: "Is everybody with a potential contribution involved?" Actively seek out people with different points of view. When you have the right group together, the leadership defines the issues. Get the group to debate and agree the agenda items – all of them – then review the agenda.

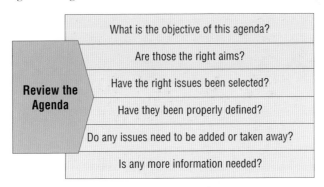

Review the Agenda

What is the objective of this agenda?

Are those the right aims?

Have the right issues been selected?

Have they been properly defined?

Do any issues need to be added or taken away?

Is any more information needed?

With these matters settled, you can start to generate alternatives and choices. Encourage everyone to speak. Aim to achieve an atmosphere in which no-one feels threatened – use humour but outlaw ridicule. Ask people to speak in rotation. When each participant has made his or her point, questions are allowed, but do not have an adversarial debate. Use agreed time limits and checkpoints to refocus the group on the main objective of the meeting. Then restart the discussions – and work together to achieve that objective.

4

The principles of leadership

How all workers (including the members of an orchestra) need leadership before management ● How principle-centered leadership confers "legitimate power" ● **10 ways to increase a leader's honour and power with others** ● Mastering the three "attitudes" and the three "behaviours" of effective communication ● **Why "abundance thinkers" have a great advantage over the "scarcity mentality"** ● Maximizing people's contribution by automation, participation in decision-making, and self-management

Stephen Covey's theories on leadership first appear in *Seven Habits* when he is discussing the second Habit ("Begin with the End in Mind"). Covey regards Habit Two as based on principles of personal leadership, of developing self-awareness and becoming responsible for the mental or "first creation". He describes leadership as a first creation that deals with the top-line question, "What are the things that I want to accomplish?" Leadership operates through the physical execution, or "second creation", which is management. Management answers the bottom-line question, "How can I best accomplish certain things?"

Covey is not, of course, alone in distinguishing between leadership and management. He cites both management guru Peter Drucker and leadership guru Warren Bennis: "Management is doing things right; leadership is doing the right things." However, times of rapid change, Covey argues, make "effective leadership more critical than it has ever been... the metamorphosis taking place in most every industry and profession demands leadership first and management second."

Not managers but leaders

He has in mind "environmental change", including market shifts so rapid "that many products and services that successfully met consumer tastes and needs a few years ago are obsolete today." So industries must "monitor the environment, including their own work teams, and exercise the creative leadership to keep headed in the right direction." Otherwise, "no amount of management expertise can keep them from failing."

This diagnosis is obviously accurate, and so is Covey's further observation: "But leadership is hard because we're

Thinker of influence

In distinguishing between leadership and management, Covey is consciously following in the footsteps of Peter Drucker. Another link between the two is time management – a Drucker speciality.

often caught in a management paradigm." To illustrate, he quotes the case of a company president who, during a year's executive development programme with Covey, realized that he "was deep into management, buried by pressing challenges and the details of day-to-day logistics". He had never "been into leadership". The man decided to withdraw from management, at the price of suffering withdrawal pains as he stopped handling detail and "started wrestling with the direction issues, the culture building issues, the deep analysis of problems, the seizing of new opportunities." His colleagues shared the pain of his withdrawal, but he reported: "I persisted.... Today our whole business is different.... We have doubled our revenues and quadrupled our profits."

Like most of Covey's discussions on business management, his distinction between managing and leading is cogent. Executives do commonly get bogged down in the day-to-day and consequently fail to pay adequate attention to the year-to-year, let alone the decade-to-decade. But *Seven Habits* does not devote significant space to organizational leadership – that is dealt with at length in *Principle-centred Leadership* (1990).

This book, derived from a Covey newsletter entitled *Executive Excellence*, is in many ways a companion volume to his great bestseller. In fact, the second chapter is actually titled "Seven Habits Revisited", and the first half of the book also includes chapters entitled "Eight Ways to Enrich Marriage and Family Relationships", and "Making Champions of Your Children". Covey sees nothing strange in this content. He criticizes people who "see no correlation between the quality of their personal lives at home and the quality of their products and services at work."

Reactive executives

Unless business people adopt the Seven Habits, they may "use a variety of ill-advised approaches in sincere attempts to improve their relationships and achieve desired results". They may well end up by turning the Seven Habits upside down, with consequences that provide, not an amusing and unrealistic caricature, but a painfully accurate description of all too many executives:

- They are reactive: they doubt themselves and blame others.
- They work without any clear end in mind.
- They do the urgent thing first.
- They think Win/Lose.
- They seek first to be understood.
- If they can't win, they compromise.
- They fear change and put off improvement.

In no way is this a model of good leadership, certainly not the "principle-centred leadership" that Covey preaches. His central point is that "Real leadership power comes from an honourable character and from the exercise of certain power tools and principles"; it does not come from genetic "great man" theories, personality "trait" theories, or behavioural "style" theories. To make his point, Covey intriguingly illuminates the different modes of leadership by looking at followers and asking: "Why do they allow themselves to be led?"

Sometimes followers have no option; they are made offers they dare not refuse. They are responding to what Covey calls coercive power. More commonly, followers follow voluntarily to earn benefits: this "may be called utility power because the power in the relationship is based on the useful exchange of goods and services". Finally, following

"To value oneself and, at the same time, subordinate oneself to higher purposes and principles is the paradoxical essence of highest humanity and the foundation of effective leadership."
Principle-centred Leadership

can be "based on the power some people have with others because others tend to believe in them and what they are trying to accomplish." This is legitimate power.

Clearly, power in organizations may well carry elements of all three of the above types. Someone with legitimate power must still satisfy his people's utility need for a good standard of living, and will probably also possess the coercive power of dismissal. Covey is disdainful of coercive power, but he accepts that utility power "is based on a sense of equity and fairness" and that, in key ways, it works well:

"Leaders are followed because it is functional for the followers. It gives them access to what the leader controls, through position or expertness or charisma. The nature of followership when based on utility power is still reactive, but the reaction tends to be positive rather than negative."

Legitimate power

For all that, utility power has limitations: "It is being increasingly acknowledged that relationships based on utility power often lead to individualism rather than teamwork and group effectiveness." Individuals are locked into a kind of perpetual bargaining as they decide what is best and right and fair. Covey contrasts this "situational ethics" with legitimate power, where "ethical behaviour is encouraged because loyalty is based on principles as they are manifested in persons."

The leader is free to make a personal choice between the three types of power. But Covey's preference for legitimate power is overwhelming: "The more a leader is honoured, respected, and generally regarded by others," he writes, "the more legitimate power he will have with others." He makes 10 suggestions "for processes and principles that will increase a leader's honour and power with others":

- Be persuasive: commit to stay in the communication process until mutually beneficial and satisfying outcomes are reached.
- Be patient: maintain a long-term perspective and stay committed to your goals in the face of short-term obstacles and resistance.
- Be gentle when dealing with vulnerabilities, disclosures, and feelings that followers might express.
- Be teachable: appreciate the different points of view, judgements, and experiences that followers may have.
- Show acceptance: withhold judgement, giving the benefit of the doubt.
- Be kind: remember the little things (which are the big things) in relationships.
- Be open: give full consideration to followers' intentions, desires, values, and goals, rather than focusing exclusively on their behaviour.
- Be compassionate: in confrontation, acknowledge errors and mistakes in a context of genuine care, concern, and warmth, making it easier for people to take risks.
- Be consistent: do not use your leadership style as a manipulative technique in order to get your own way.
- Show integrity: honestly match words and feelings with thoughts and actions.

Legitimate power also rests on effective communication. Covey states that "perception or credibility problems" are at the root of most communication difficulties. For "clearing the communication lines", he advocates adoption of six "essential" attitudes and behaviours:

- I assume good faith; I do not question your sincerity or your sanity.
- I care about our relationship and want to resolve differences.
- I am open to influence and I am prepared to change.
- I listen to understand.
- I speak to be understood.
- I start dialogue from a common point of reference or point of agreement, and move slowly into areas of disagreement.

Cynics might object that all the above add up to no more than saying that goodness is good. But Covey is a pragmatist in material things. He gives unstinting admiration to businessmen such as J. R. Simplot (1909–), who founded his wealth on selling vast quantities of potatoes to McDonald's. He links their success to one of his most prized abilities: an "abundance mentality" (see p. 56) – they share "a bone-deep belief" that natural and human resources abound to realize their dreams, and a conviction that consequently their success need not mean failure for others.

Covey contrasts this with the scarcity mentality (see p. 56), which holds that resources are limited and that success has to be won at other people's expense. "If you see

"The more principle-centred we become, the more we develop an abundance mentality, the more we love to share power and profit and recognition, and the more we are genuinely happy for the success... and good fortune of others."
Principle-centred Leadership

life as a 'zero sum' game," he comments, "you tend to think in adversarial or competitive ways, since anyone else's 'win' implies your loss." That is an insecure person's position. The abundance mentality, however, "springs from an internal security" that Covey attributes to being "principle-centred", a quality that he attaches to "abundance thinkers". He writes that thinkers such as Simplot, the potato king, share seven characteristics:

- They return often to the right sources.
- They seek solitude and enjoy nature.
- They "sharpen the saw" regularly.
- They serve others anonymously.
- They maintain a long-term intimate relationship with another person.
- They forgive themselves and others.
- They are problem solvers.

Goodness and success

It might well be objected that some highly competitive businessmen could pass all or most of these seven tests, and that Covey's heroes (he includes Ray Kroc, the forceful creator of McDonald's, and J. Willard Marriott, who built his family's hotel chain) were definitely tough in their business lives. But Covey says that there is a fundamental link between goodness and commercial success:

"In *The Seven Habits of Highly Effective People*, I suggest that the most fundamental source, and the root of all the rest, is the principle source. If our lives are centred on other sources – spouse, work, money, possession, pleasure, leader, friend, enemy, self – distortions and dependencies develop."

Hamburger hero
The late Ray Kroc, founder of McDonald's, won Covey's approval as a principle-centred entrepreneur whose "abundance thinking" is rooted in a balanced adherence to God and free enterprise.

Covey's "distortions and dependencies" create chronic problems for both individuals and organizations. Covey lists seven chronic problems that might well be called the Seven Habits of Highly Ineffective Organizations:

■ "Poor alignment between structure and shared values, between vision and systems: the structure and systems poorly serve and reinforce the strategic paths."

- "No strategic path: either the strategy is not well developed or it ineffectively expresses the mission statement and/or fails to meet the wants and needs and realities of the stream [the environment]."
- "No shared vision and values: either the organization has no mission statement or there is no deep understanding of and commitment to the mission at all levels of the organization."
- "Wrong style: the management philosophy is either incongruent with shared vision and values or the style inconsistently embodies the vision and values of the mission statement."
- "Poor skills: style does not match skills, or managers lack the skills they need to use an appropriate vision."
- "Low trust: staff has low trust, a depleted Emotional Bank Account, and that low trust results in closed communication, little problem-solving, and poor cooperation and teamwork."
- "No self-integrity: values do not equal habits; there is no correlation between what I value and believe and what I do."

Curing the problems

When Covey sees that "the senior executives want to blame everybody and everything else for those problems", they are told to look in the mirror "to identify one of the primary sources". His cure for the seven problems is to share vision and values, build all corporate activities on those solid principles, and both the organization and its people will fall into step behind one common cause, pursued with high effectiveness.

Covey backs up this argument for principle-based leadership with four basic management paradigms.

FOUR MANAGEMENT PARADIGMS

Need	Metaphor	Paradigm	Principle
Physical/economic	Stomach	Scientific authoritarian	Fairness
Social/emotional	Heart	Human relations (benevolent authoritarian)	Kindness
Psychological	Mind	Human resource	Use and development of talent
Spiritual	Spirit (whole person)	Principle-centred leadership	Meaning

Covey argues, first, that people are not motivated primarily by their quest for economic security. Second, recognizing their social needs as well "still leaves management in charge, still making the decisions and giving the commands". The third paradigm comes very near, however, to winning his outright approval:

> "When people are seen as economic, social, and psychological beings... managers try to create an environment in which people can contribute their full range of talents to the accomplishment of organizational goals."

The key word is "try". In Covey's view, managers will not fully succeed without principle-centred leadership. The fourth paradigm recognizes that people are also "spiritual beings" who "want meaning, a sense of doing something that matters". They want to "contribute to the accomplishment of worthwhile objectives". So, "Pay me well," certainly. "Treat me well," of course. "Use me well," absolutely. But above all: "Let's talk about vision and mission, roles and goals. I want to make a meaningful contribution." To that end, principle-centred leaders:

- Automate routine, boring, repetitive tasks.
- Give people a chance to take pride in their jobs.
- Encourage participation in important matters, including decision-making.
- Encourage self-direction and self-control.

Covey has a "PS Paradigm". The P stands for People. The S stands variously for Self, Style, Skills, Shared vision and principles, Structure and systems, Strategy, and Streams [operational environments]. Business management, he stresses, will under-perform and often fail unless it embraces all the S-aspects in a consistent, dynamic framework.

Ideas into action

- Concentrate first on "What are the things that I want to accomplish?"

- Delegate "management" responsibilities to leave yourself free to lead.

- Help others to believe in you and what you want to achieve.

- Look for credibility problems and make resolution of them a high priority.

- Build trust between you and those you work with on the basis of your trustworthiness, not politics.

- Ensure that you are seen as fully competent in your area of professional expertise.

- Get people to work with you on vision, mission, roles, and goals.

Managing your time

*ime is the main asset of the manager. How you allocate
time and how well you use it are the keys to effectiveness.
But time management is far more than drawing up and
keeping to schedules; you must also identify core priorities,
build in time to address non-urgent but important issues, and
learn when and how best to delegate tasks.*

Opportunity cost

A vitally important question in time management is: "What am I
doing that can only be done by me?" People rarely ask, however,
what they *should* be doing and are not: "What am I *not* doing that
can only be done by me?" Every use of time precludes, during that
use, doing something else. The concept resembles what is known in
accountancy as "opportunity cost" – the return on your money that
you lose by spending the funds on something else.

Question your approach

Covey suggests that you ask yourself two questions that force you to
think about what you do and to identify the gaps:

■ What one thing could I do (and am not doing now) that, if
done regularly, would make a tremendous positive difference in
my personal life?

■ What one thing in my business life would bring similar results?

Now use the rest of this masterclass to help you prioritize tasks,
delegate effectively, and plan your time efficiently.

STEPHEN COVEY

Benefitting from a Radical Rethink

Whatever your working role, it is likely that a radical rethink of how you
allocate your time could produce far greater personal effectiveness.

Al Zeien, the former Chief Executive
Officer of Gillette, had never thought
of conducting appraisals of his
executives. His Human Resources
advisors persuaded him – not without
some difficulty – to do so. Carrying
out 300 appraisals a year took up a
great deal of Zeien's time, but the
time spent with his staff gave him
unparalleled knowledge of his people
and the business. The partial
reallocation of the CEO's work-week
to staff appraisals made a powerful
contribution to the impressive
worldwide performance of the
company during his tenancy.

1 Picking your priorities

Covey has boiled down the principles of time management to just five words: *organize and execute around priorities*. But "Putting first things first" (Covey's Habit Three) does not mean concentrating on doing first what seems to be most urgent. You must focus on "preserving relationships and accomplishing results".

Prioritize by urgency

Some important things need not be done immediately. But this does not mean postponing them indefinitely or not doing them at all. Time management programmes, with their emphasis on efficient scheduling and control of time, often do not help in this respect. Their daily planning processes "rarely get past prioritizing the urgent, the pressing, and crisis management".

Are you addicted to urgency?

When priorities are set by urgency, responding in kind can become addictive. In fact, most managers are addicted to urgency to some degree. Has this happened to you? Find out by seeing how the following 10 statements apply. If your answer to a statement is "Never", score 0; if your answer is "Sometimes", score 2 points; if your answer is "Always", score 4.

- I do my best work under pressure.
- I am too busy to do certain things I know are important.
- I hate to wait or stand in a queue.
- I feel guilty when I take time off work.
- I seem to be rushing between places and events.
- I push people away to get on with a project.
- I feel anxious when I'm out of touch with the office.
- I am preoccupied with one thing when doing another.
- I'm at my best in a crisis.
- I think that some day I will do what I really want to.

Analysis

- 12 or below: you are probably immune from addiction to urgency.
- 13 to 24: you are vulnerable to addiction and should assess your priorities.
- 25 or above: you are addicted to urgency and should start on a cure.

STEPHEN COVEY

Analyze your use of time

Covey's Time Management Matrix (see p. 41) shows that the pattern of activities is more complex than a simple division between "urgent" and "not urgent", or "important" and "not important".

Study the matrix and then estimate what percentage of your time you spend in each of the four quadrants. Next, for three days, log how you actually spend your time, divided into 15-minute slots. Check how accurately your log compares with your estimate; the greater the discrepancy, the less your control of your time. Are you fully satisfied with the result?

Urgent and important

If you are an urgency addict, you are probably spending nearly all your time in Quadrant I – engaged in "urgent and important tasks". This inevitably means that you will not be doing enough of the "important and not urgent" tasks belonging to Quadrant II.

According to Covey, this quadrant includes seven requirements that are fundamental to good performance. Ask yourself: "Am I spending enough time on these seven important activities?"

- ■ Improving communications with other people
- ■ Preparing my activities more effectively
- ■ Improving my planning and organization
- ■ Looking after my personal business
- ■ Taking new opportunities
- ■ Developing my skills and knowledge
- ■ Empowering other people

If you are not paying enough attention to these activities, you need to change. These activities can probably be done only by you, which makes it doubly important to focus on them.

To gain time for Quadrant II activities you must take strong action in Quadrants III and IV, where activities are either unimportant or not urgent, or both. Look at the amount of time you spend in these two quadrants and ask yourself: "What tasks am I doing that need not be done at all?" Now ask yourself: "What am I doing that could be done by someone else?" You will find that many of the activities in Quadrants I, III, and IV can be undertaken just as effectively by others, lightening your own load considerably.

2 Delegating tasks

Delegating tasks appropriately is one of the most effective time savers. It enables you to concentrate on Quadrant II activities, which include empowering other people. Select tasks to delegate with care, and always plan your delegation thoroughly.

Win/Win delegation

Covey advises you to make a list of your responsibilities and then select those that can be delegated. For each task, choose people who can either do the job already or who can be trained for the purpose. Carry out the delegation of each task as soon as possible.

An effective delegation is one that results in the forging of a Win/Win agreement for both sides. Plan the delegation interview: make sure that nothing is left to chance and that both you and the delegate fully understand what is involved. Give clear guidelines on the results you expect and the time available for completion. Encourage the delegate to ask questions. Good communication between the delegate and yourself is the key to ensuring success.

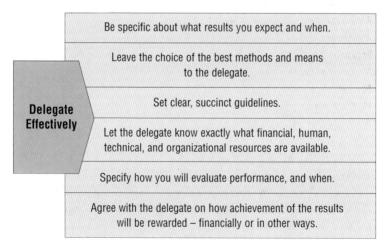

Delegate Effectively

Be specific about what results you expect and when.

Leave the choice of the best methods and means to the delegate.

Set clear, succinct guidelines.

Let the delegate know exactly what financial, human, technical, and organizational resources are available.

Specify how you will evaluate performance, and when.

Agree with the delegate on how achievement of the results will be rewarded – financially or in other ways.

Effective delegation allows you to eliminate wasted time and exploit major opportunities as they occur. You can then give a rounded management performance that includes the important things and not just those that are – or seem to be – urgent.

3 Planning each week

Every manager plays many parts, or roles, in his or her week. To ensure that you use your time effectively you must perform all the roles properly, and set goals for each of them week by week.

Identify your roles

The parts you play will vary from time to time. Study your week and write down the roles you are currently filling, both personally and professionally. The list may look something like this:

- Individual
- Spouse/parent
- Manager, global marketing
- Leader, Project Alpha
- Manager, staff development
- Manager, administration
- Chair, charity fund

Schedule your roles

Your personal life should not be squeezed into the space left after work is scheduled. Use the four-step weekly planner to ensure that you allocate plenty of time for the whole person.

The Four-Step Weekly Planner			
1 Identify roles.	**2** Set goals.	**3** Allocate time.	**4** Schedule week.

For each role you have written down, identify two or three significant goals that can be achieved in the week. Make sure that some fit into the critical "important but not urgent" category. How much time will you need to spend on achieving each goal? Now schedule that time into the week.

Covey's trademarked system is the Weekly Worksheet, which lists all the roles with their goals next to them. All goals are numbered and allocated slots in a straightforward seven-day, hour-by-hour, 8.00 a.m. to 9.00 p.m. diary. It turns out that even with as many as 17 weekday goals, seven of them allotted two hours each, you still have 41 hours of unscheduled time. Do the exercise yourself.

Review the workload

However well you plan the week, daily pressures are likely to upset the plans. Crises do occur, tasks take longer than expected, people cause unforeseen problems. You need to adapt. Take a little time at the start of each day to review the week's schedule. See what needs altering and check to ensure that you are not losing sight of your goals. You may well find that what confronts you as a particular day begins will take longer than the hours available.

Apply discipline

Covey gives the example of an executive with at least 11–12 hours of work looming ahead. How do you fit a dozen hours into eight? If you do not delegate, the usual response is to prioritize the tasks, nearly all of which will seem urgent, do as much as you can, and push the rest forward into the future. By taking a disciplined approach, however, you can control your time much better.

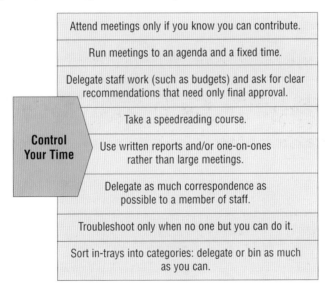

Control Your Time
Attend meetings only if you know you can contribute.
Run meetings to an agenda and a fixed time.
Delegate staff work (such as budgets) and ask for clear recommendations that need only final approval.
Take a speedreading course.
Use written reports and/or one-on-ones rather than large meetings.
Delegate as much correspondence as possible to a member of staff.
Troubleshoot only when no one but you can do it.
Sort in-trays into categories: delegate or bin as much as you can.

Above all, organize and execute around priorities, that is:

- Eliminate tasks that do not need to be done at all.
- Identify tasks that could be delegated.
- Focus on tasks that only you can do.

5

Making leadership work

Team-building: how every "cog and wheel" must work efficiently within the organization for business success ● Using the five-stage technique of "completed staff work" to tackle problems ● **The four indispensable conditions for achieving true empowerment** ● W. Edwards Deming's 14 points of quality management ● **Why "Win/Win" performance agreements are far more than job descriptions** ● Why leaders of organizations need a transformational style owever strongly Stephen Covey encourages business managers to develop lasting principles, and to use these as the engines of leadership, management comes down to making and implementing practical decisions and winning practical results – in the short, medium, and long terms. In nearly all cases, managers find that the organization, not the competition, is their main opponent, as they strive to get the right performance and the right outcomes. As Covey himself explains in *Principle-centred Leadership*:

"… the question becomes one of implementation. How can a top executive act on the 'whole person' assumption? How can the organization reflect this enlarged view of people? How can managers uproot a deeply imbedded authoritarian or benevolent authoritarian style? How can they rid the company of excess psychic and structural 'baggage' and give people the freedom and flexibility to think and act in ways consistent with this enlarged view of man?"

The second half of *Principle-centred Leadership*, dealing with "Managerial and Organizational Development", sets out to answer these questions.

Enabling staff workers

Some of the advice is eminently practical and seems self-contained; one example is the chapter on "completed staff work". The warmly endorsed principle is to have staff "think through the whole problem area, analyze the issue in depth", identify several alternatives and their consequences, and finally (and firmly) recommend one of the alternatives. Covey suggests a five-step process of enablement for these staff workers:

- Provide a clear understanding of the desired results.
- Give people a clear sense of their level of initiative.
- Clarify assumptions.
- Provide the people involved with as much time, as many resources, and as much access to other executives and departments as possible.
- Set a time and place for presenting and reviewing the completed staff work.

The chapter is less self-contained than it seems. All Covey's practical thoughts on leadership come back to the same sensible foundation: that, to "motivate people to peak performance", you should find where "organizational needs and goals overlap individual needs, goals, and capabilities". That done, Win/Win (see p. 56) agreements can be made, allowing people to "govern or supervise themselves in terms of that agreement."

Ideal empowerment

The leader/manager then serves as a "source of help", backed up by "helpful organizational systems within which self-directing, self-controlling individuals… work towards fulfilling the terms of the agreement." The

"Management must empower its people in the deepest sense and remove the barriers and obstacles that crush and defeat the inherent commitment, creativity, and quality service that people are otherwise prepared to offer."
Principle-centred Leadership

individuals also become accountable as they "evaluate themselves against the criteria specified" in that agreement. Overall, the picture is an attractive, if Utopian, portrayal of ideal "empowerment". The word means allowing people to take responsibility for their own work, which, says Covey, starts with the four indispensable conditions mentioned above:

- ▪ Win/Win agreements
- ▪ Self-supervision
- ▪ Helpful structure and systems
- ▪ Accountability

Foundations of Win/Win

The pivotal condition is the first, the Win/Win agreement. The five foundations upon which any Win/Win agreement rests are, importantly, those that also underpin any delegation that is effective (see p. 43). True empowerment follows from true delegation, and vice versa, and the five steps are all essential:

- ▪ *Specify desired results.* Discuss what results you expect. Be specific about the quantity and quality. Set budget and schedule. Commit people to getting the results, but then let them determine the best methods and means to achieve them. Set target dates or timelines for the accomplishment of your objectives.
- ▪ *Set guidelines.* Communicate whatever principles, policies, and procedures are considered essential to getting desired results. Impose as few procedures as possible to allow freedom and flexibility. Keep policy and procedure manuals brief. Guidelines should also identify

"no-nos" or failure paths that experience has identified as inimical to organizational goals or values.

■ *Identify available resources.* Identify the financial, human, technical, and organizational resources available to assist in getting desired results.

■ *Define accountability.* Specify how you will evaluate performance. Also, specify when and how progress reports are to be made and accountability sessions held. Note that when the trust level is high, people will be much tougher on themselves than an outside evaluator or manager would ever dare be.

■ *Determine the consequences.* Reach an understanding of what follows when the desired results are achieved – or not achieved. Financial and psychic rewards include recognition, appreciation, advancement, new assignments, training, flexible schedules, leaves of absence, enlarged responsibilities, perks, or promotions. Negative results lead to consequences ranging from reprimand to retraining to dismissal.

Conflicts of expectations

Performance agreements on this model are Covey's answer to all "conflicts of expectations", not only within the company but outside, with customers. If people agree on the expectations surrounding roles and goals, he argues, "management has solved many of its problems". Team-building is one internal problem. Covey likes to solve it by getting different groups together – salespeople with manufacturing or purchasing people, say – to share role-and-goal expectations in an "atmosphere that isn't emotionally charged". Get everybody's agendas on the table, he urges, and the negotiation process can begin.

The resulting Win/Win performance agreement "is much more than a job description". The latter merely lays down what the job is, and what is expected of the incumbent. Most job descriptions "have very little sense" of what constitutes a "win" for the employee, and most usually focus on external control. In contrast, the Win/Win agreement looks for internal control, to a situation where people can say "I understand, and I am committed because it is a win for me, too".

The empowered person can then practise self-supervision, which Covey presents as the antithesis of organizational control. As he says, many people see "a conflict between the need for operational integrity and the benefits of greater self-supervision." This conflict, repeated again and again, "precludes building either value, creating a downward spiral of trust that leads to cynicism, 'snoopervision', tightening control, and constant tension." Resolving the conflict can only stem from recognizing that both values are sound – in fact, they are "vital to an effective organization".

The resolution comes back to the Win/Win agreement. As people realize such an agreement, no need arises to have "some people controlling others". The organization itself – the sum of all the people – is in control, because the parts

"There's a difference between expectation and reality. An expectation is an imaginary map, a "should" map rather than an "is" map. But a lot of people think their maps are accurate, that 'This is the way it is – your map is wrong'." *Principle-centred Leadership*

"work together responsibly to create the desired results". Both the organization and its people are accountable: the organization must produce the overall results that its members desire, and they in turn must account to the organization for their self-supervised performance.

Organizational backing

Covey is aware that managers cannot go far along the route to self-supervision without organizational backing. But he has no convincing remedy for the common situation in which the manager wants to adopt these eminently sound policies, but the organization does not. Nor does Covey specify in detail how systems and structures (the fourth "condition" of empowerment) are supposed to be "helpful". It is no particular use to be told sweepingly that "All the systems within an organization must be totally integrated with and supportive of the Win/Win agreement." He does list six systems that "are common to most organizations", but mostly the listing is more aspirational than instructive:

- Information, which must be "accurate, balanced, and unbiassed".
- Compensation, which should generate both financial and self-developmental rewards, encourage synergistic cooperation, and create team spirit.
- Training and development, with the learner "responsible for the learning" and with close correlation between the training goals and individual career plans.
- Recruitment and selection, which are done carefully, matching each candidate's abilities, aptitudes, and interests with the requirements of the job.

- Job design that gives people "a clear sense of what the job is about, how it relates to the overall mission of the company, and what their personal contribution could be."
- Communication, organized around a shared vision and mission. For this, there is a longer and more specific agenda, including one-on-one visits; staff meetings with action-oriented agendas and minutes; employee suggestion schemes; open-door and due-process policies; annual interviews with the level above your immediate superior; anonymous opinion surveys; and *ad hoc* committee brainstorming.

Total Quality Management

Covey, as a highly experienced consultant, is likely to be aware that his Utopian ideals of empowerment are seldom, if ever, realized in practice, because of organizational obstacles (including unhelpful systems and structures) which, in turn, are both created by and reinforce individual prejudices. If you have managers who have not mastered the Seven Habits, the organization will not have principle-centred leadership – unless you can find a system that automatically enshrines the Seven Habits.

One of Covey's enthusiasms, in his view, promises to do precisely that: Total Quality Management (TQM). He says that "certain universal principles and purposes must be observed in order to obtain total quality of services and products." Moreover, this pursuit makes people care "about the quality of our lives and our relationships". Total Quality Management also enshrines the same principle of continuous improvement that Covey enjoins on individuals. It is "an expression of the need for continuous improvement in four areas":

- Personal and professional development
- Interpersonal relations
- Managerial effectiveness
- Organizational productivity

Covey's enthusiasm for TQM gives heroic status to the late US statistician W. Edwards Deming (1900–93). Covey calls Deming "the economic Isaiah of our time", and Deming's "14 points" are as famous in quality management as Covey's Seven Habits are in self-improvement. Deming's 14 points are as follows:

- Create constancy of purpose for the improvement of product and service.
- Adopt the new philosophy.
- Cease dependence on inspection to achieve quality.
- End the practice of awarding business on price alone.
- Improve constantly and forever the system of production and service.
- Institute training on the job.
- Institute leadership to help people and machines and gadgets to do a better job.

"Profound, sustainable, cultural change can take place within an organization… only when the individuals within the organization first change themselves from the inside out. Not only must personal change precede organizational change, but personal quality must precede organizational quality."
Principle-centred Leadership

A taste for quality

The 14 points set out by W. Edwards Deming are cited by Covey in support of his Seven Habits. Deming's writing provides a wealth of solid, down-to-earth, practical advice for management.

- Break down barriers between departments.
- Drive out fear, so that everyone may work effectively.
- Eliminate slogans, exhortations, and targets for the work force asking for zero defects and new levels of productivity.
- Eliminate work standards (quotas) on the factory floor and management by numerical goals. Substitute leadership.

- Remove barriers that rob the hourly worker of his right to pride of workmanship.
- Institute a vigorous programme of education and self-improvement.
- Put everybody to work to accomplish the transformation.

In appraising the 14 points, Covey seeks to emphasize the sovereign importance of the Seven Habits if you want to "transform the paradigms of people and organizations from reactive, control-oriented management to proactive and empowerment-oriented leadership". He clearly felt a need to link his moral philosophy with Deming's drive to raise American quality and productivity to meet the Japanese challenge in the 1970s and 1980s. That need for a linkage reflects the fact that Covey's basic programme, directed at the individual, is less easily applied to organizations.

Covey argues that his philosophy is the the "missing key" to TQM. But, if properly operated (which rarely happens), TQM is complete in itself, truly an "integrated, interdependent, and holistic" system of organizational management and corporate leadership. The adjectives are Covey's, who claims them for the Seven Habits, too.

Vast changes ahead

Covey's principles, he asserts, "when applied consistently in countless specific practices, become behaviours enabling fundamental transformations of individuals, relationships, and organizations." Transformation is required, not just to correct internal under-performance, but to respond to revolutionary external changes in virtually every industry and profession – changes so vast that, in Covey's view, they will "alter forever the way many companies operate". The changes include the shifts:

- From "brawnpower" to "brainpower".
- From mechanical to electronic technology.
- From growing birth rates to declining ones.
- From stable male workers to women, minorities, baby boomers.
- From acceptance of authoritarian, hierarchical roles to rising expectation of employee involvement.
- From externally driven/material values to internally driven/quality-of-life values.
- From a corporate drift away from dominant social/ economic values in business to the reaffirmation of those values.

Transforming management

Covey writes, "The scope and scale of these changes require leaders of organizations to adopt a transformational style." He defines this as meaning that "we change the realities of our particular world to more nearly conform to our values and ideals", and he contrasts it with "transactional leadership". The latter is concerned with "an efficient interaction with the changing realities, focusing on the "bottom-line" and centred on events. In contrast, only transformational leadership, focused on the "top line", merits the title "principle-centred".

Covey has thus quickly moved the emphasis away from real-world transformations in technologies, markets, industries, and economics and transferred it to the moral transformations that are at the heart of his doctrine. He does not explain how "building on man's need for meaning" [a transformational contribution] produces a more effective adoption of new developments – e-commerce, say – than the contrasting transactional equivalent, which might be expressed as "building on man's need to get a job done and to make a living".

In truth, transforming management to meet transformed times is one of the supreme challenges of the 21st century. But Covey has not provided a text for meeting that challenge. His concern is always with what he holds to be eternal verities, in the firm belief that they will guide leaders through any upheaval to the green pastures – and the promise of Golden Eggs – beyond.

Ideas into action

■ Allow people to govern or supervise themselves within Win/Win agreements.

■ Seek mutual understanding on expectations surrounding roles and goals.

■ Organize communication around a shared vision and mission.

■ Have subordinates write you a "manager's letter" outlining their responsibilities.

■ Organize systems for processing work that enable people to maximize their productivity.

■ Use random sampling to discover the perceptions of all customers, workers, and investors.

■ Make total quality a prime concern and objective for the business.

Exchanging teaching for business

Stephen Covey's decision to leave Brigham Young University, after 20 years as a professor, changed the direction of his career — but not of his philosophy. By that time, it was formed and ready for a wider audience.

As a colleague, Blaine Lee, recalls it, Covey had "plans for affecting management in America" by applying the principles that were to be enshrined in *The Seven Habits of Highly Effective People*. Initially, Lee was contracted to spend a year training and coaching Covey's "handful of professionals". The year went so well that Lee promptly joined Covey as one of the owners who, in 1984, turned Stephen Covey and Associates into the Covey Leadership Center.

Even before the publication of *Seven Habits* in 1989, the new company gave Covey an indispensable vehicle. On his own, he could never have spread his ideas, or earned income from corporate customers, anything like so widely. He simultaneously created a valuable business asset: the Center was named as one of America's fastest-growing private companies in 1994. While a few other gurus have followed similar strategies, none has played the corporate game more successfully than Covey, whose pathfinding included rapid expansion into overseas markets. In 1994, Covey was International Entrepreneur of the Year.

The Center, led by like-minded associates such as Lee, several of them authors or part-authors of books themselves, institutionalized Covey's evangelism. He focused this on "teaching the transforming power of principles or natural laws that govern human and organizational effectiveness". The Center was basically a people business on both sides of the equation: people teaching people, rather than people selling products.

Commercial gains

Franklin Quest, however, had achieved an equal reputation as a purveyor of products, led by the Franklin Day Planner, a bestselling time-management tool. When *Seven Habits* spent five consecutive years (1991–95) as America's top non-fiction bestseller, the door opened to

massive brand exploitation, from *The Seven Habits Family Collection* to *Loving Reminders for Couples* (not to mention *for Kids*). The complementary nature of the two businesses seemed to create a natural fit, and they were duly merged in June 1997. The combined company is far more than Stephen Covey writ large – although its chairman, Hyrum Smith (above, at left), formerly boss of Franklin Quest, is another man after Covey's heart, author of *The 10 Natural Laws of Successful Time and Life Management*.

Since the company was already publicly quoted, the merger gave Covey an automatic path to stock market wealth. The path has not been smooth, however. In 1999 the share price

"Once people have experienced real synergy, they are never quite the same again. They know the possibility of having other such mind-expanding adventures in the future."
The Seven Habits of Highly Effective People

fell by over half; a Utah commentator explained that the "management continues to battle to integrate the operations of the two companies". Since Habit Seven is "Synergize", that integration should have proved simple enough for a Covey company. Practice and preaching do not always move in step, but Covey's crucial gain is already accomplished – the message has new, multi-million dollar muscle.

GLOSSARY

ABUNDANCE MENTALITY: Belief that there is plenty of potential reward for everybody in any business relationship: opposed to the SCARCITY MENTALITY (see below).

AFFIRMATION: A statement that helps an individual or organization to approach an event with clearly stated purposes and policies.

CHARACTER ETHIC: System of belief and behaviour founded on enduring moral principles.

CIRCLE OF CONCERN: All issues that impinge on a person's life and work.

CIRCLE OF INFLUENCE: Those issues within the CIRCLE OF CONCERN that one can directly affect.

COMPLETED STAFF WORK: Delegating an entire problem to staff, who return with a full and final recommendation.

CREATION: The "first creation" is mental, forming a plan (the function of leadership); the "second creation" is executing the plan (the function of management).

EMOTIONAL BANK ACCOUNT: Metaphor for the amount of trust built up or withdrawn in a relationship.

EMPATHY: Seeing things from the other person's viewpoint, as in "empathetic listening".

"GOFER": A subordinate deprived of responsibility who is ordered to "go for" this and "go for" that.

HABIT: Development of knowledge, skill, and ambition to achieve characteristic, effective behaviour.

MATURITY CONTINUUM: Successive development of habits to pass from dependence through independence to interdependence.

MISSION STATEMENT: Setting out priorities, values, and objectives for a person or an organization.

PARADIGM: Basic mental framework – the vision of the world of an individual or organization – that strongly influences ideas and actions.

P/PC BALANCE: Optimizing by balancing the highest possible Production consistent with the fullest development of the means of production, Production Capability.

PROACTIVE: Taking the initiative to make things happen and taking responsibility for one's own behaviour: the opposite of REACTIVE.

REACTIVE: Merely reacting to events as they occur, and trying to shift responsibility to others.

SCARCITY MENTALITY: Belief that one person's gain must of necessity be another person's loss.

SELF-FULFILLING PROPHECY: Taking action that makes a forecast outcome inevitable.

"SHARPEN THE SAW": Metaphor for regular exercise and practice to maintain and improve personal performance.

SYNERGY: Working with others to achieve a combined and therefore superior outcome.

TOTAL QUALITY MANAGEMENT (TQM): A set of long-term techniques and practices designed to continuously improve the quality of all products and processes.

UTILITY POWER: The usual economic relationship in which individuals exchange their time, work, and talents for the organization's pay and benefits.

VISUALIZATION: Performance-enhancing technique in which a future event is envisaged beforehand to strengthen the ability to obtain desired results.

WIN/WIN: Seeking or agreeing a plan of action that promises equal satisfaction to both parties.

BIBLIOGRAPHY

The core of Stephen Covey's literary output is *The Seven Habits of Highly Effective People*. This mammoth bestseller is essential to understanding Covey's philosophy of personal and business life. It has also provided the theme for books and other publications (tapes, videos, etc) on Covey's second area of concern, the family and interfamilial relationships.

Covey's *The Seven Habits of Highly Effective Families* led to a companion book by his son Sean, *The Seven Habits of Highly Effective Teens*. The Covey stable, built around the former Covey Leadership Center, has also produced works like *The Power Principle* by Blaine Lee and the co-authored *First Things First*, another Covey bestseller. This book sprang from the discovery that Habit Three, "Put First Things First", with its emphasis on time management, was the most neglected of the seven.

More strictly a business book than *Seven Habits*, although overlapping with it significantly, *Principle-centred Leadership* bears the marks of its origin in a series of newsletter articles. Business and workplace matters also account for a third of *Living the Seven Habits*, a collection of "stories of courage and inspiration" that relates Covey's teaching to real-life experiences. Another book, *The Nature of Leadership*, explores Covey's principles through interviews and photographs.

WORKS CITED

Sean Covey (1999) *The Seven Habits of Highly Effective Teens*,
　　Simon & Schuster UK Ltd, London
Stephen R. Covey
－ (1989) *The Seven Habits of Highly Effective People*,
　　　　Simon & Schuster UK Ltd, London
－ (1990) *Principle-centred Leadership*, Simon & Schuster UK Ltd, London
－ (1994) *Daily Reflections for Highly Effective People*,
　　　　Simon & Schuster UK Ltd, London
－ (1997) *First Things First Every Day*, Simon & Schuster UK Ltd, London
－ (1998) *Balancing Work and Family*, Covey Leadership Center, Utah
－ (1998) *The Nature of Leadership*, Franklin Covey, Utah
－ (1998) *The Seven Habits Family Journal*, Covey Leadership Center, Utah
－ (1998) *The Seven Habits of Highly Effective Families*,
　　　　Simon & Schuster UK Ltd, London
－ (1999) *Living the Seven Habits*, Simon & Schuster UK Ltd, London
Stephen R. Covey, A. Roger Merrill with Rebecca R. Merrill (1994)
　　First Things First, Simon & Schuster UK Ltd, London
Blaine Lee (1997) *The Power Principle*, Simon & Schuster UK Ltd, London

Index

Robert Heller

Robert Heller is himself a prolific author of management books. The first, *The Naked Manager*, published in 1972, established Heller as an iconoclastic, wide-ranging guide to managerial excellence – and incompetence. Heller has drawn on the extensive knowledge of managers and management acquired as the founding editor of *Management Today*, Britain's premier business magazine, which he headed for 25 years. Books such as *The Supermanagers* and *In Search of European Excellence* address the ways in which the latest ideas on change, quality, and motivation are providing new routes to business success. In 1990 Heller wrote *Culture Shock*, one of the first books to describe how IT would revolutionize management. Since then, as writer, lecturer, and consultant, Heller has continued to tell managers how to "Ride the Revolution", the title of his 2000 book, written with Paul Spenley. His books for Dorling Kindersley's Essential Managers series are international bestsellers.